THE MIGHTY BLACKHAWKS

2010 STANLEY CUP CHAMPIONS

CHICAGO SUN-TIMES

Chicago Sun-Times

Publisher
John Barron

Editor in chief
Don Hayner

Project Editor
Craig Newman

Sports Editor
Chris De Luca

Contributing Writers
Rick Morrissey
Mark Potash
Adam L. Jahns
Mark Konkol
Rick Telander
Neil Hayes
Kyle Koster

KCI Sports Publishing

Publisher
Peter J. Clark

Managing Editor
Molly Voorheis

Book and Cover Design
Nicky Brillowski

ISBN: 0-9843882-4-9 (PB)
ISBN: 0-9843882-6-5 (HC)

Printed in the United States of America
KCI Sports Publishing   3340 Whiting Avenue, Suite 5   Stevens Point, WI 54481
Phone: 1-800-697-3756   Fax: 715-344-2668
www.kcisports.com

FOREWORD By Rick Morrisey, Chicago Sun-Times

It's one thing to be a favorite to win a title. It's another to actually win one. And it's something completely different to win one in Chicago, which isn't known as a destination spot for trophies looking to settle down.

Thin as it might be, an argument can be made that, in 2006, the Blackhawks were the most woeful of Chicago sports franchises. Sure, there were the Cubs and that whole century-of-futility thing closing in. It's hard to get past the round number of 100.

But the Hawks seemed to be living in another century, and there was considerable evidence that the century was the 19th. No games on television, per the dictates of owner Bill Wirtz. Not a lot of money being spent on players. Fans treating the United Center as if it were the Asbestos Center. No Stanley Cup title since 1961.

At least the Cubs had day games and sunshine.

The Hawks were an indoor funeral procession.

Above: The celebration is on for the Blackhawks, 2010 Stanley Cup champions, and their fans.
Tom Cruze | Sun-Times

Less than four years later, on June 9, 2010, the Hawks — the mighty Blackhawks — beat the Philadelphia Flyers to win the Stanley Cup.

Is the phrase "Miracle on Ice" already taken?

The Hawks won the Cup because of the talent and youthfulness of Jonathan Toews and Patrick Kane; the missing teeth of Duncan Keith; the doggedness of Marian Hossa; the steady hand and impressive mustache of coach Joel Quenneville; and the resolve of owner Rocky Wirtz, who opened a window and let fresh air blow in.

They won because of Patrick Sharp, Brent Seabrook, Kris Versteeg, Brian Campbell, Tomas Kopecky, Andrew Ladd, Troy Brouwer, Brent Sopel, Antti Niemi, Dave Bolland, Dustin Byfuglien, Ben Eager, Niklas Hjalmarsson, John Madden, Cristobal Huet, Adam Burish, Colin Fraser, Jordan Hendry and Nick Boynton.

How it happened is a story of death and life.

It started with the drafting of Toews and Kane, in 2006 and 2007, respectively, thanks to the eye of former general manager Dale Tallon and his staff. It was like John Lennon and Paul McCartney meeting for the first time in Liverpool. OK, maybe not that momentous, but you get the idea. Both players made their Hawks' debut in 2007. In terms of personnel decisions, whatever happened before or after for the Hawks is, by definition, secondary.

FOREWORD

When Wirtz died in September 2007, his son, Rocky took over, and like the road less traveled, it made all the difference. That is not disrespect for the dead, just the truth. One of the first things Rocky Wirtz did was to hire former Cubs president John McDonough as Hawks president. And just like that, all the things that had held back the franchise were no longer constraints.

The games started appearing on television. Long-time fans had to rub their eyes to believe what they were seeing. McDonough worked hard to bring back disgusted fans. He had Toews and Kane do every media interview and make every public appearance possible.

And Tallon continued adding players to a core that already included Keith, Seabrook, Bolland, Byfuglien and Sharp. Hossa was brought in. So were Madden and Kopecky.

All of it — the players, the coaching, the business decisions — led to the Hawks' first Stanley Cup in almost a half-century.

So many memories from a championship season.

Kane's artistry with the puck on his stick, his mouth guard hanging halfway out of his mouth like a fishhook.

Hossa's overtime game-winner against Nashville in the first round of the playoffs after Kane had tied the game with 13.6 seconds left in regulation.

Toews' relentlessness on both ends of the ice.

Bolland's ability to be in the right place at the right time. His ability to irritate the bejabbers out of opponents.

Sharp's professionalism and scoring ability.

Byfuglien's emergence in the playoffs. His nasty hit on Chris Pronger, the Flagrant Flyer, in Game 5 of the Stanley Cup finals.

Eager's fury.

Brouwer's improvement in the playoffs after learning his father was recovering nicely from a blood clot in his brain.

Huet's help in getting the Hawks to where they wanted to go. Niemi's cool demeanor in the face of thousands of doubters in the playoffs.

Jim Cornelison's regular losing battle at singing the national anthem over a roaring United Center crowd. Sources say he has a wonderful voice.

And perhaps the most lasting image of these Hawks, Keith's mouth after he was hit by a puck in the Western Conference finals against San Jose. He ended up missing only seven minutes of ice time — one minute for each missing tooth — while getting treated.

That's why the Hawks won the Stanley Cup. It was a refusal to take no for an answer. It was the hockey that mattered, and for all the good business decisions Wirtz made to turn around the franchise, the hockey was the thing.

The Hawks were a marvelously talented team. They went four lines deep, and that was legit, not talk. And it's not hyperbole to look at Kane, 21, and Toews, 22, and envision Hall of Fame induction speeches from them someday.

But that's for much, much later. The Hawks will have some salary-cap decisions to make in the off-season, but they are in position to be very, very good for a long time. Is it too early to be thinking about multiple Stanley Cup titles? Too greedy?

Probably. You never know about the future, especially in a sport of funny bounces and in a city of not-so-funny occurrences. So fully enjoy this one, Chicago.

But no one will blame you for peeking ahead.■

CONTENTS

Chicago Blackhawk players line up for the National Anthem as the ice is now painted with the Stanley Cup Playoff logo. Scott Stewart | Sun-Times

STANLEY PLAYOFFS CUP

WESTERN CONFERENCE QUARTERFINALS

GAME 1: PREDATORS 4 / BLACKHAWKS 1

The Blackhawks knew what to expect.

They knew the Nashville Predators play a trapping, check-first game. And they knew things reach another level in the Stanley Cup playoffs — and that anything is possible.

So maybe that's why there weren't too many feelings of surprise — or anger — in the Hawks' locker room after the Predators rallied for a 4-1 win Friday in Game 1 of their best-of-seven Western Conference quarterfinal series at the United Center.

Above: *For fans that came into the playoffs with high hopes, a 4-1 Game 1 thumping from the Nashville Predators offered no reason to celebrate.* Scott Stewart | Sun-Times

The Predators' J.P. Dumont had two goals — including a bouncing soft score that tied the game at 1 early in the third period and the eventual game-winner on a rebound seconds after he forced a turnover.

Jerred Smithson and Martin Erat each scored on an empty net for Nashville, the seventh seed in the Western Conference. Patrick Kane scored the Hawks' lone goal.

"Chicago has a lot of power and it's a tough building to play in, but we managed to keep battling and kept up the pressure and came away with the win," Dumont said. "We worked hard the whole game and got stronger as it went along."

Dumont, a former Hawk, scored the decisive goal when he forced a turnover by Troy

Above: Brent Sopel hangs his head in front of a quieted crowd after the Blackhawks were shocked by the Predators. Scott Stewart / Sun-Times

Brouwer, got the puck to David Legwand and then scored on a rebound.

"The third period was a tough one," Hawks coach Joel Quenneville said. "We lost a bit of our momentum on the first goal, but the second one was a tough one to give up. We had possession, had fresh legs, and turned it over in a critical spot.

"They play a hard game, and they play simple, and they can frustrate you. We got a little out of our game after they got the lead. We can be better than that."

The Hawks had their chances, but Predators goalie Pekka Rinne was there to turn them away or their defensemen were able knock the puck away.

Kane gave the Hawks a 1-0 lead at 9:43 in the second period when he crashed the net

and put in a rebound of a shot by Sharp.

"We had quality chances," Sharp said. "Give their goaltender credit. Give their team defense credit for clearing pucks out of the front of the net. ... The goal we did score was just a simple shot from the outside with a guy going to the net. That's a playoff goal right there. We have to get grittier and dirtier and find a way to get more of those."

Dumont's first goal will go down as the momentum stealer. It seemed to catch Antti Niemi off guard and gave the Predators "some belief," Nashville coach Barry Trotz said.

Dumont called it a "lucky bounce."

"We were a little rusty but that lucky goal in the third period got us going and built our confidence," Trotz said. "We had a solid third period and found a way to win."∎

Above: Chicago Blackhawks forward Andrew Ladd takes a quick shot on Nashville Preadtors goalie Pekka Rinne, who came up big constantly in the game. *Scott Stewart | Sun-Times*

Jim Cornelison almost surely sang the word "brave" at the end of his rendition of the "Star-Spangled Banner" on Friday night, though given the crowd's traditional mission to drown out his every word, who could tell?

For all we know, he might have sung "home of the worthless and weak" or, if he had a death wish, "home of the Nashville Predators."

It was loud at the United Center for Step 1 of the Blackhawks' playoff journey, and then, for the longest time, it wasn't loud at all. The Predators didn't get a lot of quality shots on goal, but they did dominate the puck for stretches in the first period.

Looking back, it couldn't have been more ominous.

Looking ahead, it doesn't look particularly sunny, not after the way Nashville had its way in a 4-1 victory in Game 1 of this first-round playoff series.

As the night wore on, the uneasy silence of the United Center gave way to grumbles.

Here's a wakeup call: Unless the Blackhawks decide it's important to knock their opponent off the puck and into the parking lot, this is going to be a very unhappy series.

NO QUIT IN NASHVILLE

For the Hawks, Friday was like one of those dreams where you're falling helplessly. They ... couldn't ... get ... the ... puck ... out ... of ... their ... zone.

Patrick Kane finally — finally — got them on the board with a rebound of a Patrick Sharp shot midway through the second period.

It was 1-0 Hawks. You could almost feel the sigh of relief inside the gray structure on Madison Street.

It wasn't that the Hawks had been flat until that point. It was that the Predators wouldn't go away. They were relentless. Still, in terms of Nashville actually scoring a goal, the color-coded threat level seemed to be a pastel.

How wrong that turned out to be.

The Predators tied the score when Hawks goalie Antti Niemi misplayed a tricky hopper from J.P. Dumont 1 minute, 31 seconds into the third period. Bottom line: Niemi has to make that save.

The second goal wasn't his fault. It was caused by the same problem that had dogged the Hawks all night: They couldn't get out of their end. Troy Brouwer lost the puck as he made his way toward his own blue line, the Predators' David Legwand got a shot off and Dumont knocked in the rebound midway through the third.

The final two goals were empty-netters in the last minute of the game. Emptiness is the feeling of the moment for the Hawks.

"They play a hard game, and they play simple, and they can — frustrate you," coach Joel Quenneville said. "We got a little out of our game after they got the lead; we can be better than that."

'IT'S PARITY'

Many of the 22,256 who showed up Friday had come to see a bloodletting. What they saw instead was a finger picking at a scab.

Most of them had seen or heard about the opening-game upsets in the other first-round series and surely were worried about adding to the trend.

Turns out they had reason to be worried.

"It's parity," said Nashville coach Barry Trotz, whose seventh-seeded team beat a No. 2 seed. "There are a lot of good teams."

The Predators had to be positively tickled by how things started, even if they couldn't actually get a goal out of it. A 0-0 tie after one period? Where do they sign up for that?

The Hawks' best scoring chance in the first came on Sharp's breakaway, which was thwarted by Nashville goalie Pekka Rinne.

Speaking of Finnish goalies who were making their Stanley Cup playoffs debut, the Chicago version probably is going to take grief for Friday's opener. Niemi's performance won't and shouldn't relieve jittery Hawks fans. It's going to take at least a series to earn their trust and even then, if Roberto Luongo happened to walk by, they might drop to their knees and declare their undying love.

But most of the bad things that happened Friday night weren't Niemi's doing. He was good enough to get his team a victory.

Nashville outshot the Hawks 13-4 in the last period.

Among the many things Niemi and the Hawks have going for them in the playoffs is the United Center. It has its own energy. But it was nervous energy Friday, and the vibe wasn't good. The vibe said, "Uh-oh."

Now it's up to the Hawks to live up to the enthusiasm of their audience in Game 2 on Sunday.

"We have a lot of respect for what they can do," Sharp said of the Predators. "The regular-season points and standings don't mean anything right now, and we need to find a way to beat these guys on Sunday."

There are huge expectations on these Hawks, and maybe what happened Friday night is the result. Better to get it out of the system now.

The playoff beards are in their infancy, and Kane's playoff mullet is in its glory. What more could your standard-issue Hawks fan want? A victory, of course.

More than that, a reason to breathe easier. ■

Dave Bolland may not garner the spotlight as much as his teammates.

But his success could be a huge spark for the Blackhawks in the playoffs.

Bolland is the center on the second line with Patrick Kane and Troy Brouwer and has taken over the left point on the first power-play unit, which will need to put up big numbers if the Hawks hope to advance. The Hawks were 0-for-2 on the power play against the Predators.

"I played the point in juniors," said Bolland, who also sees time on the penalty kill. "I like that spot. ... You can create a lot of things off there. I know I've got to be careful. I can't get too low in the offensive zone because I've got to get back just in case someone is flying. ... But I like it. I can do some damage there."

Bolland is looking at the playoffs as a "new beginning" after returning from back surgery on Feb. 3 and struggling to find his stride in the regular season.

Bolland was paired with Marian Hossa when he returned, but after coach Joel Quenneville altered his lines, Bolland appears to have more chemistry with Kane.

"He is improving," Quenneville said. "He can add so much to this team with his positioning and his thought process with and without the puck."

THIRD-LINE RINGERS

Kris Versteeg has played with Andrew Ladd and John Madden on the third line throughout the year.

But Versteeg has never given much thought to the fact he is playing with two Stanley Cup champions — until Friday.

"Now that you mention it,"

Above: *Nashville Predator J.P. Dumont scores on Blackhawks goaltender Antti Niemi in what would be the game-winner.* Scott Stewart | Sun-Times

Versteeg said. "It is pretty cool."

The benefits of playing with Ladd and Madden in the playoffs are obvious to Versteeg.

"They know what it's all about and what it takes," Versteeg said.

"And they tell me all the time what you have to do to be successful. It's exciting to skate out there with two guys who know what it takes to win."

MULLET STORY

Kane's mullet haircut earned him a new nickname in the Hawks dressing room.

"'Joe Dirt' has been coming out a lot," Kane said. "That's the name around here. It's almost like you hear 'Hey, Joe!' in the locker room and you got to look — that's for me."

The idea behind the mullet, which Kane added "steps" to above each ear, is to keep things loose during the postseason.

"Sometimes it's fun to do something for the playoffs like this," said Kane, who scored the Hawks' only goal Friday. "If it's not working for the team or myself, then I'm going to have to do something different." ∎

WESTERN CONFERENCE QUARTERFINALS

GAME 2:   PREDATORS 0 / BLACKHAWKS 2

Blackhawks coach Joel Quenneville made it very clear what was needed from his team to even its Western Conference quarterfinal series with the Nashville Predators.

"We're asking everybody to add a little more to what we did Friday night — knowing that it wasn't good enough," he said.

That meant playing a full 60 minutes, being physical in all areas, getting as much traffic as possible in front of Nashville goalie Pekka Rinne and converting on the power play.

And although Game 2 at times felt a lot like their Game 1 defeat, the

Above: *Blackhawks fans finally had a chance to whoop it up after Chicago evened things up in Game 2.* Tom Cruze | Sun-Times

Hawks were able to accomplish most of what was needed for a 2-0 win against the Predators on Sunday night at the United Center.

Antti Niemi made 23 saves for the Hawks' first playoff shutout since Ed Belfour in 1996. Patrick Kane scored and had an assist, and Dave Bolland had a power-play goal as the Hawks evened the series at 1-1.

"We went in hungry," said captain Jonathan Toews, who also had an assist. "It was kind of shocking a little bit to not come out on top in that first game. We wanted to get a better start in Game 1, especially at home with our crowd. We wanted to take advantage of those games here, and we expected to win that first one.

"Coming out of that, we knew there were a lot of things that we could do better. As individuals, every guy looked at themselves and

Above: As rough as goalie Antti Niemi was in Game 1, he was a stone wall in the Hawks' Game 2 win. Here he makes a first period save against Nashville winger Joel Ward. Tom Cruze | Sun-Times

knew that there were some things we could each do better. We all showed up to play tonight and chipped in."

No player showed up more than Niemi. As in Game 1, the Predators were able to maintain pressure in the attacking zone, especially early in the second period, and the Hawks struggled to clear the puck.

But Niemi showed no signs of being affected by the Friday loss by turning away the Predators every time Sunday, including tough stops on Dustin Boyd and Jordin Tootoo.

"Antti came up with some critical saves," Quenneville said.

Three penalties helped negate any steam the Predators had in the second period as Bolland scored at 8:44 on the power play. It was important that the Hawks took advantage, especially since during 5-on-5 play the Predators were able to fend off most attacks

with their trap system and continued to cycle the puck well offensively.

"They play a pinching game and just wait for us to make mistakes,"

Bolland said. "They were ... taking it to us.

"In all these series, PP goals are the ones that get you ahead. ...

That's where you have to capitalize."

Kane scored the all-important second goal just over four minutes into the third period, and the Hawks needed a strong penalty-killing effort to put away the Preds, who won Game 1 with a strong third.

"We were focused and ready to go before that third," Toews said.

"We were very conscious of what happened last game going in with a 1-0 lead."

The Predators played without leading scorer Patric Hornqvist (undisclosed injury).■

What, you worry? No, not you, Mr. and Mrs. Blackhawks Fan. Oh, goodness, no. I would never imply that. You had complete confidence in your team even before its 2-0 victory over the Nashville Predators on Sunday night.

But there were people who looked very much like you sweating bullets early in Game 2 at the United Center. Uncannily like you.

Halfway through the first period, many in the crowd already were openly frustrated. Jonathan Toews had an open shot that smacked off the crossbar, and the groans hit the ceiling with a thud.

When an official waved off Dave Bolland's goal, saying it came after the whistle, there seemed to be a general consensus among the fans that the unfortunate had crossed the line into the criminal.

Coach Joel Quenneville was staring death rays at the officials.

I believe the fans were chanting "bull spit," but I could be wrong.

And yet, given their poor performance in a 4-1 loss in Game 1, the Hawks had to be heartened by how they were playing Sunday.

They were getting scoring chances, even if it wasn't translating into goals.

They were keeping the puck in the Predators' zone, something that hadn't been true Friday night. By the time the first period was over, the Hawks had outshot Nashville 13-5.

For the second game in a row, goalie Antti Niemi was playing well.

All of the good things that were going on for the Hawks finally paid off on a power-play goal by Bolland in the second. Patrick Kane passed the puck into the slot to Toews, who pushed it to Bolland, whose backhander beat Predators goalie Pekka Rinne.

So the question was whether you could trust that goal. Was the lead real? The Hawks had been stunned by the Game 1 loss, and the fact that they had scored first in that contest only added to their shock. During the regular season, they were 40-9-7 when they scored the first goal of the game.

Was it real? Yes. In the third, Kane picked up a loose puck, made his way up the right side, made Predators defenseman Kevin Klein commit to the possibility of a pass to Patrick Sharp, then beat Rinne with a wicked wrist shot.

Chicago breathed again.

NO SENSE OF PANIC

With the series tied 1-1, the people with an emotional stake in this team can get back to thinking about world dominance. After the Game 1 loss, everyone around here seemed to lose his or her strut.

"We knew there was a lot of things we could do better as individuals," Toews said. "I think every guy looked at themselves and knew that there were some things we could each do better. We all showed up to play tonight and chipped in."

Most of the pressure rested on the Hawks, and rather than call

Nashville winger Steve Sullivan and Hawks winger Tomas Kopecky exchange pleasantries. Tom Cruze | Sun-Times

Sunday a must-win for the home team, as some analysts had, the more appropriate term would have been a "mustn't-lose" game. That's how

it feels when the stress is squeezing your breathing passages.

But the Hawks insisted they weren't feeling any pressure going into this one.

"Nobody's panicking here," forward Kris Versteeg told reporters Sunday morning. "But you definitely don't want to go down 2-0.

Everyone knows that, but there's no panic button or anything like that. We're confident with what we can do."

The Hawks were scoreless after one period, but so were the Predators. It had a much different feel than Game 1. On Friday, a heaviness seemed to settle over the ice and in the legs of the Hawks, who looked as if they were fighting gravity as much as they were the Predators. If the NHL kept time of possession the way the NFL does, Nashville would have dominated.

Before this game, the Hawks had talked about getting more traffic in front of Rinne, and at times Sunday night, it looked like the Eisenhower during construction.

Quenneville switched up some of his lines Sunday and put defensemen Duncan Keith and Brent Seabrook back together.

MORE GAS IN THE TANK

Hockey players and coaches like to talk about the importance of having time and space to make a play with the puck. A loss Sunday would have meant that time and space were running out for the Hawks in this series.

Now everything has changed.

"Much better effort," Kane said. "I think we've still got more in the tank."

There were times when the Hawks reverted to their Game 1 sin of looking for the perfect pass and the perfect shot on the power play. You wanted someone, anyone to shoot the blessed puck. Sort of hard to score when you don't. Even a bad shot can lead to a good rebound.

But they outshot Nashville 13-7 in the second period and figured if they kept up the assault of pucks, it would pay off. And it did with Kane's goal.

Niemi was outstanding, stopping 23 shots. He made a wonderful sliding save to deny Dustin Boyd about three minutes into the second period.

"There was more energy with our team," Quenneville said.

Call it what you want — energy, life — but the Hawks are breathing easier. ∎

PATRICK KANE

The capacity crowd at the United Center might have been getting nervous. But Patrick Kane was as cool as he could be.

"I know from being a fan of the Sabres for so long, I was one of those kids jumping up and down on the couch, kind of screaming at them, 'Beat the puck out of the zone!' Or 'Score on the power play!'" he said.

"But as a player, you're a little bit more even-keeled and low-key and you know things can change and you can change them yourself. As a fan, that's just the way you are."

With an uncomfortable feeling hovering over the UC as the Blackhawks protected a 1-0 lead against the Nashville Predators early in the third period of Game 2 of their Western Conference quarterfinal, Kane took matters into his own hands Sunday night, putting the crowd at ease and the Hawks back on track.

Taking full advantage of a three-on-one break, Kane fired a shot past Nashville goaltender Pekka Rinne with 15:42 left in the third period for an insurance goal of immeasurable import. With a two-goal lead, the Hawks finally had the gritty Predators where they wanted them and used the momentum to cruise to a critical 2-0 victory.

"Coming out of the locker room for the third period, I knew we had to play to win and not play to tie," said Kane, who also assisted on Dave Bolland's goal in the second period. "Maybe the third period the last game, we gave up an unlucky goal and kind of tightened up. You get that second goal and everybody is a little looser and playing with more confidence."

Above: The Blackhawks had much more to celebrate in Game 2, this time cheering Dave Bolland's first period goal to give them a 1-0 lead.
Tom Cruze | Sun-Times

Kane's goal was set up by Patrick Sharp, who poked the puck past a Nashville player along the boards near center ice and straight to Kane, who came charging in from the right side, with Sharp and Bolland also bearing down on Rinne.

Kane played it perfectly, hesitating just enough to give himself a clear shot. He rifled a wrist shot past Rinne from 15 feet for a 2-0 lead.

"I was thinking pass the whole way, actual-ly," Kane said. "As soon as I got the puck, I was thinking pass. It's one of those things where it's a split decision. You change your mind, especially with a guy like Sharp there. On a three-on-one, you have him back door, and he's probably going to bury that nine times out of 10. But I was looking at Sharp the whole time. Maybe the goalie thought I was going there and just looked up, and I shot where I thought I was open."■

Above: *The Blackhawks salute the fans after the team's Game 2 win over the Nashville Predators.* Tom Cruze | Sun-Times

★ THREE STARS ★

★ ANTTI NIEMI
Without Niemi, the Hawks would have been in trouble. He came through with several key stops in the second period, including one on Dustin Boyd with his outstretched leg. It was the first Hawks shutout in the playoffs since 1996.

★ PATRICK KANE
The winger scored the Hawks' second goal and assisted on Dave Bolland's power-play goal. Kane looked off Pekka Rinne on a 3-on-1 breakout, then scored with a wrist shot at 4:18 in the third.

★ PEKKA RINNE
Rinne (31 saves) made several big stops for the Predators and prevented the Hawks from breaking it open. He yielded few rebounds and robbed Marian Hossa on the power play in the second.

Above: *Patrick Sharp celebrates after Patrick Kane's 3rd period goal gave the Blackhawks a 2-0 lead.* Tom Cruze | Sun-Times

WESTERN CONFERENCE QUARTERFINALS

GAME 3:   BLACKHAWKS 1 / PREDATORS 4

The Nashville Predators' energy was overwhelming, their emotion overpowering, their hits punishing and their home crowd deafening.

And the end result was absolutely crushing for the Blackhawks.

The Hawks lost to the Predators 4-1 on Tuesday in Game 3 of their Western Conference quarterfinal series at Bridgestone Arena. The Predators lead the best-of-seven series 2-1, with Game 4 scheduled for Thursday.

"Certainly tonight, we can't be pleased with the way we played," Hawks coach Joel Quenneville said. "They were the harder-working team, more resilient, more desperate. We know that each and every game it is going to escalate, and today, for whatever the reasons, we didn't achieve what we wanted to."

Matching and surpassing the emotion and energy of the Predators were absolute musts for the Hawks to win Game 3, Quenneville said before the game. Afterward, he said the Hawks' competitiveness is "absolutely" one thing he will have to address after they were outshot 35-27 and outhit 32-18.

"We knew it was going to be tough coming

Chicago Blackhawks right wing Marian Hossa falls after colliding with Nashville Predators defenseman Shea Weber.   Mark Humphrey | AP Photo

into this building," Hawks winger Patrick Sharp said. "They played well in front of their fans. They brought a lot of energy.

"It would be nice to see some urgency. I think guys played hard, but we can get it up another level."

David Legwand had a goal and two assists, and Joel Ward and Shea Weber also scored for the Predators. Martin Erat capped the victory by scoring on a penalty shot in the third period.

Tomas Kopecky scored on a power play with 2:25 left in the first period for the

Above: *Chicago Blackhawks goalie Antti Niemi, of Finland, blocks a shot against the Nashville Predators in the first period.* Mark Humphrey | AP Photo

Hawks, who appeared to have cut off the Predators early momentum by tying the score at 1.

But the Predators didn't let up, scoring twice in the second period. Legwand scored on a nice setup from Steve Sullivan, and Weber's slap shot deflected off Marian Hossa's stick and through goalie Antti Niemi's legs.

Pekka Rinne stood out again for the Predators in net. He made 26 saves, including one on Kris Versteeg from in close after Versteeg had stick-handled past defenseman Dan Hamhuis.

The Hawks' penalty-killers and Niemi were able to foil the Predators on three power plays in a row in the first period. But it was only a minor victory in a battle ultimately won by the more physical Predators. Niemi finished with 31 saves.

"We didn't meet the necessary emotion for the game," Quenneville said.

The Predators established the physical play in the first period and used it to incite their already-rowdy home crowd. Weber sent Patrick Kane falling to the ice with a hard check into the boards, and Francis Bouillon leveled Colin Fraser in front of the Hawks' bench.

The hits ultimately set the tone for the one-sided game.

"Every game, we've got to play desperate now," Hawks captain Jonathan Toews said. "There is no more time to wait."∎

There's nothing fluky about this. In fact, it looks very much like the better team is winning this series.

That would be the Predators, the mighty Predators. And unless something changes quickly and dramatically, the Blackhawks could soon be on an extended spring break, their playoff beards gone after a few millimeters of growth.

Nashville dominated them in a 4-1 victory Tuesday night and took a 2-1 lead in their best-of-seven first-round series.

"They were definitely the harder-working team, more resilient, more desperate," Hawks coach Joel Quenneville said.

This isn't just about the Hawks playing poorly, though there was a lot of that Tuesday. The Predators are good with the puck in traffic. They're good at holding on to the puck behind the Hawks' net.

They're just good.

And the Hawks did little to make things difficult for Nashville puck-handlers. It looked too much like a skills competition. They might want to think about hitting somebody, even if just for pride's sake.

On Tuesday, the Predators had so many more quality scoring opportunities, you would have been forgiven for thinking they were the heavily favored team.

Over and over again, they got to the puck first. Here's the problem: I'm not sure the Hawks even know how to beat the Predators to the puck. For starters, it would be nice if Jonathan Toews and Marian Hossa showed up.

"It doesn't come down to one thing necessarily," forward Patrick Sharp said. "I guess if you had to put your finger on it, it would be hard work and getting dirty."

Tuesday a fluke? No.

According to NHL.com, since 1994, the seventh seed has beaten the second seed 46.3 percent of the time. Think about that. The team that had enough talent, toughness and cohesion to finish with the second-most points in the conference beats what appears statistically to be the vastly weaker opponent only about half the time.

In the NBA, the better teams during the regular season almost always win against the lesser teams in the playoffs. The No. 8 seed Bulls have about as much chance of beating the top-seeded Cavaliers as a pauper does of dating one of the Kardashian sisters.

LeBron James can take over the fourth quarter of a playoff game, as he did to the Bulls on Monday night, but it's not a given that the best players on the ice in an NHL game will take over the third period. Washington's Alex Ovechkin didn't get off a single shot in Game 1 of the No. 1-seed Capitals' series against No. 8 Montreal.

That little stat about the No. 2-No. 7 seed is the numerical proof of what we saw with our own eyes in the first two games. This series was no gimme for the Hawks. This was going to be a hard slog.

What makes what happened in the first two games even more surprising -- or scary -- is that the Hawk voted Most Likely to Cost His Team the Series, goalie Antti Niemi, was excellent.

Heading into Game 3, he led the league in playoff goals-against average (1.01) and playoff save percentage (.957).

And he wasn't the problem in Game 3, either.

The problem? It might come down to something Nashville coach Barry Trotz said recently.

"We have to want it more than them," he said. "You break the game down to the primitive baseline, and it comes down to one-on-one battles. The guy that's standing right next to you? You've got to be better than him. We need a lot of our guys to be better than their guys."

Sounds simplistic, even silly. But maybe there's something about hockey that gives an inferior athlete the chance to beat a better athlete. Or maybe the Predators do indeed want it more than the Hawks, who have been told most of the season that they are prime Stanley Cup contenders. Maybe the Hawks thought they could skip several steps on the way to the championship series.

Maybe they were mentally planning the parade route.

"We didn't meet the necessary emotion for the game," Quenneville said Tuesday night.

Talk about an incriminating statement.

It was 1-1 after one period, and it reinforced the idea that the Predators are for real and that the Hawks are in for the fight of their lives. Besides dominating the puck for extended periods, they pushed around the Hawks. Predators defenseman Francis Bouillon hit Colin Fraser so hard that officials hoped to retrieve the black box to find out what happened.

That led up to the first goal, a back-handed rebound by Joel Ward to put Nashville up 1-0. Niemi seemed to be under constant attack.

The Hawks tied it on a power-play goal late in the first. Tomas Kopecky scored on a backhander from in front of the net.

The Predators scored two goals, one off a two-on-one and another on a cannon by Shea Weber from just inside the blue line, to take a 3-1 lead in the second. And that, for all practical purposes, was the game.

The series wasn't supposed to be like this, but it is. The Hawks knew it after a 4-1 Game 1 loss, and they knew after a closely fought victory in Game 2.

Game 4 is Thursday. Maybe they'll show up for this one. ∎

Above: *Marian Hossa skates to the bench after Shea Weber scored in the second period.* Mark Humphrey | AP Photo

★ THREE STARS ★

★ DAVID LEGWAND
The veteran center was in the middle of every-thing, most of it benefitting the Predators. He scored the tie-breaking and momentum-turning goal early in the second period off a pass from Steve Sullivan and assisted on the Predators' two other goals.

★ STEVE SULLIVAN
The ex-Blackhawks forward has been a bigger factor in each game. He burned the Hawks badly with a rush down the right side, then fed Legwand for an easy goal that gave the Predators a 2-1 lead. Also assisted on Joel Ward's first-period goal.

★ PEKKA RINNE
He continued to stymie the Hawks with another solid effort in goal. The 6-5 Finn faced mostly minor resistance from the sloppy Hawks but stopped 25 of 26 shots, allowing only Tomas Kopecky's power-play goal in the first period.

ADAM BURISH

Adam Burish can't save the world. And he probably can't save the Blackhawks all by himself.

But at least he'll let the Predators know they're not playing the Herbivores.

Barring a bad case of brain lock tonight on the part of coach Joel Quenneville, Burish will find himself back on the ice, where he should have been all along in this Western Conference playoff series.

The things the Hawks have missed the most in the first three games are the exact things Burish offers: toughness, hard work and a tendency to annoy the daylights out of the opposing team.

After their 4-1 loss in Game 3 on Tuesday night, the Hawks agreed that the Predators outworked them. How that is possible is almost unfathomable, given that these are the playoffs and that the Hawks are considered one of the favorites to make it to the Stanley Cup finals.

Effort would seem to be a given. And maybe that's the assumption Quenneville made when he decided not to dress Burish for the first three games. Everyone would work hard, right?

After two losses to the seventh-seeded Predators, Quenneville apparently has seen the light: Not everyone has Burish's fight.

And that's why Burish was practicing on a line with Troy Brouwer and John Madden on Wednesday afternoon. It looks as if Bryan Bickell will be playing in Game 4, too, though Quenneville wouldn't say anything definitive about anyone, presumably out of national security concerns, presumably Canada's. He was mum about defenseman Brian Campbell as well, but it's hard to believe Campbell will play tonight when even sneezing hurts his ribs.

The Hawks would love to have Campbell's speed on rushes up the ice.

But at this point, what Burish offers might be more important to the playoff life of this team. To say the Hawks are near death is silly. To call them unresponsive in their loss Tuesday is a little closer to the truth.

"Like 'Q' said at our meeting Wednesday morning: We have to have more urgency," Burish said. "We didn't have that urgency to our game, and in the playoffs you have to have that. They dictated

Above: *Blackhawk right winger Adam Burish sticks his tongue out as he anticipates a hard shot from Columbus Blue Jackets defenseman Anton Stralman.* Tom Cruze | Sun-Times

the pace, and they kind of controlled the physical play of the game."

It has become obvious after three games that the Hawks need someone to knock the Predators off the puck. Unless you're a fan of watching a team play keep-away, the moment calls for someone to announce he's not going to take it anymore. That should be Burish, who does not like the idea of the master (Nashville) drawing back the Milk-Bone from the expectant dog (your Blackhawks) over and over again.

Sometimes, it's just not pretty.

"To win games in the playoffs, it's not always just about your skills," Burish said. "It's not about making the pretty play. It's about who's going to

So maybe the message arrived a little late. OK, maybe the message arrived a lot late, two losses late.

But the important thing is that it didn't come back marked "undeliverable" this time.

After looking listless and almost unrecognizable in Game 3, the Blackhawks finally came to life in a 3-0 victory over the Predators on Thursday night.

This playoff series is tied 2-2, and there's every reason to think the Hawks perhaps, possibly, might have come out of their funk.

For a team with Stanley Cup aspirations, the idea that it would take this long to get emotionally involved might seem hard to believe, but that's where the Hawks were heading into this huge game.

Whether the pilot light will stay on for the rest of the playoffs is an unknown, but it was good to see it burning brightly with the Hawks in such a precarious position.

Energy, urgency, desire, desperation, will — whatever you want to call it — they had it Thursday. They came out of the locker room in a dark and stormy mood. They finally lived coach Joel Quenneville's catchphrases.

Traffic in front of the net? Check.

Abrasiveness? Check.

There was so much at stake.

"You never want to say must- win this early," forward Patrick Sharp said.

"It was a must-win for us to stay alive," Jonathan Toews said.

For the first time in the series, the Predators weren't the only team getting to loose pucks. And the Hawks finally decided they were going to punish Nashville players for thinking they could pass the puck around with impunity.

"We had groups of three guys up front that were skating at all times and helping each other out," Toews said. "Tuesday night, sometimes maybe we had one or two guys watching the other guy work.

When we checked and created loose pucks in their end, we never really had a second or third guy picking up that puck and creating plays. But Thursday we did."

MOB ACTION PAYS OFF

The Hawks scored their first goal when they mobbed the net on a power play in the open-ing period. Patrick Kane took two shots in close before Sharp put back a rebound.

Quenneville had Adam Burish and Bryan Bickell in the lineup for the first time this series, the hope being that they would add much-needed passion to a team he said had been outworked in Game 3.

The very act was just as important as anything any of those particular players brought to the ice. The message was that the so-called stars needed emotional rescue.

Among those who were found alive and well Thursday was Toews, who scored his first goal of the series. That gave the Hawks a 2-0 lead and some breathing room. But the most heartening thing is that they kept charging.

Sharp snapped a wrist shot past Predators goalie Pekka Rinne to make it 3-0 in the second.

You want to say the Hawks will take off from here, but you wanted to say that after Antti Niemi's 2-0 shutout in Game 2, didn't you?

But they looked like a different team Thursday, which is to say they looked like their old selves.

Maybe they had read the comments of ESPN analyst Barry Melrose in the local newspaper here: "It just appears to me that the Predators want it more than the Hawks. Last season, the Hawks were a very gritty team, very hard to play against and very physical. I don't see that now. ... They're playing like they don't want to get their noses dirty."

The last thing a hockey player wants to be called is a blue blood.

A hockey player doesn't want to be told he puts his skates on over silk stockings.

Niemi had his second shutout of this series. The last Hawk goalie to do that was Tony Esposito in 1974. Remember how much handwringing there had been over Niemi heading into the playoffs?

It looks kind of silly right now.

And while we're skating down memory lane, remember when defenseman Brian Campbell was considered wildly overpaid, a result of former general manager Dale Tallon's foolishness? What a waste of skating speed, everyone said.

CAMPBELL SHOWS HIS GRIT

But Hawks fans were waiting with bated breath for his return. Turns out the guy can play a little bit. He came back Thursday after missing almost six weeks because of a broken collarbone and rib.

Somewhere along the way, there was a change of heart about Campbell. Few defensemen can skate the way he can, and that became painfully apparent after Alex Ovechkin mashed him into the boards.

He probably came back earlier than he should have, but these are the playoffs. Maybe his attitude rubbed off on his teammates.

"I felt comfortable battling," Campbell said. "I felt strong. But it was definitely a huge challenge to get back in there. Mentally, I really worked on it the last day and a half. It's tough because you don't know how you're going to react and how it's going to feel."

So maybe this is the game in which the Hawks woke up for good.

We'll see. But it wasn't hard to see why they won this one.

"What's the difference?" Predators coach Barry Trotz said.

"Sometimes it's just urgency."

There's that word again. Urgency. What's the other one? Energy.

"I thought we skated a little bit better this game and came out with that energy and enthusiasm," Sharp said.

Enthusiasm. That's a new one. It fits too.∎

BRIAN CAMPBELL

For Brian Campbell, it was a chance worth taking. What is life without risks?

The veteran Blackhawks defenseman was expected to miss eight weeks after suffering a broken collarbone when he was driven into the boards by Alex Ovechkin of the Washington Capitals on March 14. But with the Hawks trailing the Nashville Predators 2-1 in their Western Conference quarterfinal series, Campbell decided to return to the ice two weeks early.

Even with Campbell's ice time limited, It probably was not a coincidence that the Hawks played their best game of the series with him on the ice, beating the Predators 3-0 on Thursday at Bridgestone Arena.

"If we were ahead in the series I don't think I would have played," Campbell said. "But I felt like I was ready and I could help the team. We'd all like to have eight weeks to get ready. But we might not have eight weeks. I thought it was key to get back."

Campbell played 14:04 in the game and had extensive ice time in the third period, when the Hawks were protecting a 3-0 lead.

"I felt great, especially in the third period," Campbell said. "The first period was a little foggy. I haven't played in six weeks — coming back to playoff hockey, they come at you pretty good. It was a challenge. I didn't play a lot in the first two periods, but in the third I felt comfortable."

Even though he didn't figure in the scoring, Campbell's presence on the ice gave the Hawks a lift.

"I think it did, and I'm not being a cocky person," he said. "But Adam Burish and myself, we've been around, we've been through a playoff run with these guys. We were so excited to be back, we were chirping away before the game, getting the boys going.

"Everybody wants to see everybody playing. I went through 68 games with these guys. Adam fought back hard from an injury that kept him out all year. They love seeing that."

"We were excited to have Soupy back in the lineup," Blackhawks coach Joel Quenneville said. "He did a great job in his first game back, worked his way through the first period and got better and better with each shift. For his first game in a long time he did a remarkable job."

Campbell hopes to build on the momentum in Game 5 on Saturday.

"We've got to continue that," he said. "Tonight we played desperate playoff hockey. And we have to keep responding every night.∎

Blackhawks defenseman Brian Campbell plays a little more than six weeks after breaking his collarbone and a rib after a hit from Washington's Alex Ovechkin. Mark Humphrey | AP Photo

WESTERN CONFERENCE QUARTERFINALS

GAME 5: PREDATORS 4 / BLACKHAWKS 5 (OT)

The seconds are ticking off as fast as your heart is beating, your opponent has an extra man on the ice, one of your most dynamic players is sitting helplessly in the penalty box and your season is teetering on the brink of near-conclusion.

Yes, coach Joel Quenneville and the rest of the Blackhawks certainly could have done without the emotions of their roller-coaster-of-a-ride 5-4 overtime win against the Nashville Predators on Saturday in Game 5 of the Western Conference quarterfinals at the United Center.

But they'll take them, all of them — especially Patrick Kane and Marian Hossa, who scored the biggest goals in the biggest win for the Hawks this season.

Kane had a short-handed goal with 13.6 seconds left in regulation to force overtime, and Hossa scored the game-winner at 4:07 into OT — 11 seconds after he left the box following a five-minute major boarding penalty — against the Predators.

The most important thing is that the Hawks have a 3-2 edge in the series and can advance to the conference semifinals with a win Monday night in Nashville, Tenn.

"The feeling you have right now after win-

Above: Blackhawks hockey fans go wild after Marian Hossa potted the game-winning goal in overtime. *Scott Stewart | Sun-Times*

ning and the feeling you had on the ice after with the towels coming down and the place just roaring, it was really indescribable and unbelievable," Kane said.

"I don't even remember the play. It just kind of came on my stick."

For Hossa, who was assessed a five-minute major penalty for shoving Predators defenseman Dan Hamhuis into the boards with 1:03 remaining, sitting in the penalty box during the final stages of the victory transformed from absolute torture into pure elation.

"You don't want to know what was going through my mind in the penalty box," Hossa

Above: Antti Niemi has NHL Linsman Mark Shewchyk check his hockey pants after the puck disappeared on a shot. Scott Stewart | Sun-Times

said. "It was a really long five minutes in the box. When I saw ... Patrick score the goal, I was jumping in the cage like a little kid. Another four minutes into overtime ... what a relief when I saw the puck coming to me, and I put it in."

Hossa's game-winner capped a near-disastrous game by the Hawks in which they led 3-1 before Nashville scored three in a row to take a 4-3 lead on Martin Erat's second goal at 11:39 of the third. Joel Ward's short-handed score late in the second started the Predators' rally.

Still, the Hawks' penalty-killers, as they have been all series, were the difference down the stretch.

Nashville had a good chance to pull out the win by beginning overtime with nearly four minutes left on Hossa's penalty. But the Hawks' penalty kill, led by forwards John Madden and Dave Bolland and defensemen Niklas Hjalmarsson and Brent Sopel, stood its ground.

All four were on the ice when Hossa tapped in the winner off a shot by Sopel. The Hawks have yet to allow a power-play goal to the Predators in this series.

"It was a huge obstacle to overcome not just in overtime but to get the equalizer," Quenneville said. "It was a pretty dramatic turn of events. We all like the win. We all like to get ourselves in a better position, but we had the game in a pretty good spot there at 3-1. ... The whole thing was pretty remarkable."

Kane, Hossa and Hjalmarsson each had a goal and an assist. Andrew Ladd and Tomas Kopecky also scored, and Jonathan Toews and Brent Seabrook each had two assists for the Hawks, who took advantage of an errant centering pass by Erat to come up with Kane's equalizer.

Antti Niemi made five saves in overtime for the win.

"You have to be willing to play right to the end against Nashville," Quenneville said. "It was a little bit too dramatic for me today. But certainly at the end of the day, we like the result."∎

Marian Hossa

Playoff heroes don't come much more sheepish than Marian Hossa on Saturday.

"What can I say?" were the very apt first words out of Hossa's mouth in his postgame interview after scoring the winning goal in the Blackhawks' improbable 5-4 overtime victory against the Nashville Predators in Game 5 of their first-round playoff at the United Center.

If it were up to the Predators, "Sorry about that," would be a pretty good start. Hossa and the Hawks turned garbage into gold like few players and teams have in playoff hockey. How often does a five-minute major that could lead to a suspension spark the offending team to victory?

"What a relief," Hossa said.

In a span of 30 minutes, Hossa went from a guy who couldn't buy a break to the luckiest man in the playoffs. His major penalty for checking the Predators' Dan Hamhuis into the boards with 1:03 left in regulation looked like

Above: Tomas Kopecky celebrtaes with teammate Jonathan Toews (19) after Kopeckey scores to give the Blackhawks a 3-1 lead. Scott Stewart | Sun-Times

Opposite Page: Marian Hossa scores and celebrates the game-winning goal in over-time. Scott Stewart | Sun-Times

★ THREE STARS ★

★ PATRICK KANE
His knack for scoring big goals in big games was never more important than on Saturday. A short-handed goal with 13.6 seconds left in regulation? That will be tough to top. Kane now has three goals and three assists in the series.

★ MARIAN HOSSA
Even during a frustrating series, he's been trying to do the little things to make an impact. Finally, a little thing led to a big thing — after hustling out of the penalty box in over-time, he was in the right place at the right time and scored the winning goal.

★ MARTIN ERAT
Opportunistic forward has typified the Predators' impressive resiliency in this series. He scored two third-period goals on his only two shots of the game to turn a 3-2 deficit into a 4-3 lead that nearly held up. He has four goals on 11 shots in the series.

the clinching blow in a discouraging defeat.

Instead, the short-handed Blackhawks tied the game with 13.6 seconds left in regulation on Patrick Kane's rebound goal. After Hossa's teammates fended off the final 3:57 of his penalty to go 21-for-21 in penalty killing in the series, Hossa scored the game-winning goal by hustling out of the penalty box, setting up in front of the Predators net and waiting for Brent Sopel's shot to deflect off the stick of Nashville's Joel Ward right to him.

"It was a huge break," said Hossa, who had not scored on his first 16 shots in the series. "I was looking for something like this.

"It was one of the longest times I've ever sat in the penalty box, that's for sure — especially in a game like this. But the guys on the penalty-killing unit deserve lots of credit. The lucky rebound came to me, and I just pretty much had an open net and put it in."

Hossa can only hope his luck hasn't run out because he could face an immediate suspension for his hit, and the Predators are calling for one. They were comparing it to Alex Ovechkin's hit on Brian Campbell that led to Ovechkin being suspended for two games.

"I don't even know the difference," Predators coach Barry Trotz said. "But the league will handle it. I trust the league's judgment."

Hossa claimed the hit was unavoidable but seemed to know that a suspension is possible.

"I cannot worry about it," he said. "That's up to them. I tried to go for the puck. Hamhuis turned his back to me, and I couldn't stop. I didn't want to hit him like that. But you can't stop your motion."

Hawks coach Joel Quenneville thought the big issue was whether it was a minor or major penalty.

"He's got the puck. He's sideways. It's not from behind," he said of Hamhuis. "We don't think it was ... you argue that it was. But it was a remarkable thing that we ended up having success off of it."∎

WESTERN CONFERENCE QUARTERFINALS

GAME 6: BLACKHAWKS 5 / PREDATORS 3

Gone are the trapping, never-out-of-it Nashville Predators. Hello, Sedin twins, Roberto Luongo and the Vancouver Canucks — again.

The Hawks eliminated the Predators from Stanley Cup contention with a 5-3 victory in Game 6 of the Western Conference quarterfinals Monday at Bridgestone Arena. The Hawks won the first-round series 4-2 and advanced to play the Canucks for the second consecutive year.

Patrick Sharp and Jonathan Toews each had a goal and two assists, and Duncan Keith had a goal and an assist. Toews' power-play goal with 31 seconds left in the first period was the difference as the Hawks' penalty-killers shut the door again.

Chicago Blackhawks right wing Tomas Kopecky, center, celebrates a goal by teammate Duncan Keith, not shown, during the first period. Defending for the Predators are Joel Ward (29), Dan Hamhuis (2), and Marcel Goc (9), of Germany. Mark Humphrey | AP Photo

"Whenever you can win a playoff series, especially against a team like Nashville, it feels good," Sharp said. "I don't know who said it was going to be an easy series or we were going to get upset. It was two teams that played hard going back to the regular season. It was a very tough series. I give them a lot of credit. It could have really gone either way."

Patrick Kane was credited with a fluky goal in the first after an attempted dump-in by Brent Seabrook (two assists) ricocheted off his skate and past an out-of-the-net Pekka Rinne

(27 saves). Marian Hossa had three assists, and John Madden scored an empty-net goal.

"Nashville wasn't an easy opponent, that's for sure," said Hossa, who was booed every time he touched the puck for his Game 5 shove on defenseman Dan Hamhuis. "They play really well, especially defensively. It's really hard to play against them, and they deserve a lot of credit. We never really had an easy time against them like some people may have thought."

The seven goals in the opening period were

Chicago Blackhawks defenseman Brent Sopel, center, and Dustin Byfuglien, right, congratulate goalie Antti Niemi after the Blackhawks beat the Nashville Predators 5-3 in Game 6. The Blackhawks won the series 4-2.

Mark Humphrey | AP Photo

more than the single-game totals of the first four games of the series — as the up-and-down emotions from Game 5 carried over. The Hawks had a chance to extend their 4-3 first-period lead in the second but failed to despite a four-minute power play.

The Hawks had expected a spirited, desperate opponent and were able to match it. The last thing the Hawks wanted was a Game 7.

"You want to win every series, and we wanted to finish it off tonight," Brent Sopel said. "We didn't want to go back for Game 7 because Game 7 you never know what can happen."

The Hawks' penalty killing was at its best again when it mattered most — and despite allowing its first goal of the series. Down a goal, the Predators had three power plays in the third period, including two penalties on the shot-blocking Sopel.

But only a few shots with the advantage actually reached goalie Antti Niemi, who recovered from a shaky start to shut out the Predators in the second and third periods. Niemi finished with 25 saves, after allowing three goals on nine shots in the first.

"It was a really a tough time to be on the penalty kill," Toews said. "If you give them one there, it gives them a lot of momentum and gives them a lot of energy, thinking that they can win."

As in Game 5, the Hawks had a 3-1 lead. But Nashville rallied, keeping the puck in the Hawks' zone, being physical and scoring on the power play for once.

Jason Arnott's power-play goal at 15:44 in the first period ended an 0-for-22 streak against the Hawks in the series. Arnott had two goals in the first period and Shea Weber scored and had an assist.

Nashville's end-to-end competitiveness in the series didn't surprise the Hawks, who expect another one with the Canucks.

"There's never an easy round in this business," coach Joel Quenneville said. "The challenges obviously go up. But the first round is always a tough round." ■

GRINDERS RELISH DIRTY WORK

Blackhawks wingers Bryan Bickell and Tomas Kopecky don't mind all the shoving, whacking or even the occasional stick in the back.

In Bickell's case, he's not even bothered by the black right eye he earned battling for a puck with Nashville Predators standout defenseman Ryan Suter.

"He got me in the corner," Bickell said Monday before Game 6. "Playoff hockey, that's what it is all about."

Bickell and Kopecky have assumed the dirtier but necessary roles on the Hawks' first and second lines. It's their job to dig out pucks from the corner, battle defensemen and fight for space in front of the net.

"I love it. I love those little battles," said Kopecky, who plays with Patrick Sharp and Marian Hossa on the second line. "It's something I learned from the best in the Detroit Red Wings' Tomas

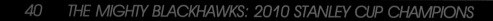

Holmstrom.

"Those are the kinds of plays where everybody is throwing the pucks at the net, even from the corners, and there are loose pucks. You're going to score the goals from there."

Traffic in front of Predators goalie Pekka Rinne was lacking early in the Western Conference quarterfinal series, and Joel Quenneville opted to change his lineup because of it. Now every line has a player — Bickell, Kopecky, Andrew Ladd and Troy Brouwer — to provide it.

The 6-4, 223-pound Bickell was put on the top line with Patrick Kane and Jonathan Toews, and Kopecky moved up from the fourth. The changes worked for a victory in Game 4 and helped the Hawks take an early lead in Game 5.

Kopecky didn't record a point on the Hawks' first goal Monday, but he was definitely a major factor. He screened Rinne and actually appeared to tip Duncan Keith's shot. Bickell made his playoff debut in Game 4, and he had a plus-1 rating in Game 6.

"Somebody's got to do the dirty work, and I don't mind it being me," Bickell said.∎

Antti Niemi lets out a yell after the Blackhawks scored an open-net goal. Mark Humphrey | AP Photo

HOLD SERVE AND PROTECT; HAWKS ADVANCE BUT LOSE SOME LUSTER

Jonathan Toews was making no apologies for the way the Blackhawks survived the Nashville Predators when they had the chance to dominate them. A win's a win. But a blown 3-1 lead is a blown 3-1 lead.

"We're hoping that's nowhere near our best," Toews said after the Hawks' uneven but effective 5-3 victory over the Predators clinched their Western Conference quarterfinal series 4-2 on Monday at Bridgestone Arena. "We've got a long ways to go.

"We found a way to win. Everybody expected us to make it through this series, but you can't expect to win four games in a row. We'll keep getting better every day and have fun with it."

Give the Hawks credit for fighting through a difficult series against an unbelievably resilient opponent and doing all they needed to do at this time of year: advance to the next series. But the Nashville series also left plenty of cause for concern. In a series where the Hawks were desperately looking for a chance to

take control, they blew two golden opportunities to put the hammer down in Games 5 and 6. In both games, they lost 3-1 leads before rallying to win.

And Monday night's clincher poured cold water on the idea that the Hawks were forced into a taffy-pull by an inferior team dragging them down to their level. The Hawks finally got the shootout they wanted, the lead they wanted, the break they wanted — and still

couldn't put away the Predators until John Madden's empty-net goal with eight seconds left made it 5-3.

The Hawks might still be the Stanley Cup contenders they're purported to be. But this series didn't state their case.

"It would have been nice to protect some leads," Hawks center Patrick Sharp said, "and it would have been nice to put them away in some games. But give credit to Nashville. They didn't go away.

It was one of the toughest series I've played in as a pro. It definitely wasn't easy."

Hawks coach Joel Quenneville noted that first-round games often are the toughest to play. But it's unusual for a team to struggle too much and still go all the way.

By winning Game 6, the Hawks avoided putting themselves in a tough fight against history. The last team to be taken to seven games in the conference quarterfinals and still win the Stanley Cup was the Pittsburgh Penguins in 1992 — that's the year the Penguins struggled to beat the Capitals in seven games in the first round but eventually swept the Hawks in the Stanley Cup finals.

The Hawks are a young, talented — and mercurial — team. They're capable of anything. But as this series showed, that capability can go both ways. The Hawks managed to fend off the Predators in their building. But they also struggled to beat a team that played most

of the series without their best offensive player, Patric Hornqvist. Just saying.

"They're a tough team to play against, especially in their own building," Toews said. "We found ways to weather the storm. We tried to stall them and bring everybody back their way whenever they tried to throw everything they had at us. So we give ourselves a lot of credit for playing that way."

The point is, this series left a big question about this team: Just how good is it? They go into a series against Vancouver with a totally different dynamic — one that could allow them to show just how good they really are.

"We're on a nice roll right now," Toews said. "We're happy about that. The game the other night Game 5, yeah, we blew a lead. It's not the way you're supposed to win a game. But at the same time, it's playoff hockey, and anything can happen."

Coming off a series that often was as difficult to watch as it was to play, that's a good thing to keep in mind. Anything can happen.■

Above: Martin Erat (10) of the Nashville Predators races John Madden (11) of the Chicago Blackhawks for the puck. Frederick Breedon | Getty Images

★ THREE STARS ★

★ JONATHAN TOEWS
Captain had a goal and two assists and was a plus-2 in the game. He came through at a critical time with a rebound goal to give the Hawks a 4-3 lead with 31 seconds left in the first period after the Predators had rallied from a 3-1 deficit into a 3-3 tie.

★ BRENT SOPEL
Earned high praise from Predators coach Barry Trotz with another solid defensive performance. Led the Hawks with five blocked shots and was a plus-1 to finish plus-4 for the series.

★ PATRICK SHARP
Had a goal and two assists and was a plus-1. His goal in the first period gave the Hawks a 3-1 lead. Also assisted on Toews' tiebreaking goal late in the first period that proved to be the difference.

MARIAN HOSSA

Above: Winger Marian Hossa works in the offensive zone against the Vancouver Canucks. Tom Cruze | Sun-Times

Marian Hossa, unsung hero? Not exactly the role even Hossa envisioned after signing a 12-year, $62.8 million contract with the Blackhawks in the offseason. A two-time All-Star forward, Hossa came to Chicago averaging 36 goals in his previous nine NHL seasons.

After scoring 24 goals in 57 regular-season games, Hossa has been invaluable in the playoffs with his forechecking, speed and puck control and by aggressively attacking the net — all factors that have made the Hawks the best team in the playoffs. Hossa leads the team with a plus-7 postseason rating.

But he has scored two goals in 14 postseason games. That's not a big deal when the Hawks are getting scoring from every line.

Hossa's coaches and teammates couldn't be happier with his contributions. But Hossa could.

"It's definitely bugging me when the puck's not going in," he said, "because I like to do better scoring goals, and things aren't going my way right now. It is in my head. But I try not to put too much pressure on myself because it's not going to do any good, right?"

Hossa is playing hard and getting shots on goal. All he can do is keep shooting and hope to catch a break.

Above: Hawk right winger Marian Hossa during warmups. Tom Cruze | Sun-Times

"Sometimes it's a little thing," he said. "Just a little break when the puck goes off your shin pad or something like that, and all of a sudden you score another one and things are going your way."

But those breaks can be hard to come by. With an empty net in the final 90 seconds of the Hawks' 4-2 victory in Game 2 on Tuesday night, Hossa made an aggressive move toward the net, but his shot from the right side hit the post. Moments later, Patrick Sharp gave up a chance for an empty-net goal and passed to Hossa at the blue line for what looked like a sure thing. But Hossa was offside.

Still, it was another good game for the 31-year-old Slovakian winger. With the Hawks leading 3-1 in the third period, his steal led to Niklas Hjalmarsson's slap shot that Troy Brouwer redirected to all but clinch the outcome.

Hossa's all-around excellence might be a surprise to those who know him as a shooter. He said he has picked up his forecheck-ing in recent years and learned from "two of the best" in Pavel Datsyuk and Henrik Zetterberg with the Red Wings last season. "It fits my style," Hossa said.

At some point, Hossa's scor-ing could become an issue. He's not being paid $7.9 million a year to forecheck. But with the Hawks on a roll, it's hard to dis-pute coach Joel Quenneville's satisfaction with Hossa's "total contribution."

"Five-on-five responsibility, offensive zone, defensive zone — rock-solid," Quenneville said of Hossa. "Kills penalties, power play. He gives us a lot of puck possession, as well. His thought process of how he plays our sys-tem is as good as anybody. We appreciate the way he plays and contributes. Goal-scoring can go up and down. But a guy like that can break out any night and be a big factor."∎

Patrick Kane hits the ice before the start of the game. Scott Stewart | Sun-Times

WESTERN CONFERENCE SEMIFINALS

GAME 1:   CANUCKS 5 | BLACKHAWKS 1

The Vancouver Canucks buried the Blackhawks with an onslaught Saturday night. But it all started in goal.

"We're obviously a great team when Roberto's playing like that," defenseman Kevin Bieksa said after Roberto Luongo stopped 36 of 37 shots in the Canucks' 5-1 victory in Game 1 of their Western Conference semifinal series at the United Center. "We can weather a lot of storms. He keeps us in the game and allows our offense to take over."

The Canucks' stunning victory was a perfect example of how lethal that game plan can be. Luongo stymied the Hawks at the outset — stopping 17 shots in the first period, including a breakaway by Patrick Kane and big saves on Jonathan Toews, Dustin Byfuglien and John Madden.

"It was nice to start that way," Luongo said. "I hadn't played in a week. It was nice to get that kind of work early in the game to get that comfort level back right away. After that, it felt like normal."

Above: Steve and Derek Persky from Palatine are ready for Game 1 against the Canucks.
Scott Stewart | Sun-Times

After Mason Raymond's back-breaking goal with 10.5 seconds left in the first period and Henrik Sedin's goal in the first minute of the second period gave the Canucks a 3-0 lead, Luongo's job was a lot easier. He allowed only Kane's goal on a 5-on-3 power play early in the third period after the Canucks led 5-0.

It was a big difference from his last playoff game at the UC when Luongo was crestfallen after allowing seven goals — four in the third

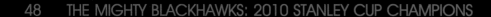

Above: The Blackhawks bench is in shock after the Vancouver Canucks scored five goals in Game 1. Scott Stewart | Sun-Times

period — in a 7-5 loss that eliminated the Canucks. But Luongo said he didn't feel any personal redemption.

"Nothing. It means nothing to me," he said. "It's only one game.

We're here to win four games, not one. There's no satisfaction for me personally or for this team."

Despite some contentious games last year in the playoffs and during the regular season, the Canucks were determined to play hockey Saturday night.

"Don't get me wrong, we still hate them," Bieksa said. "But it's more important to win the game. We thought the disciplined approach would better serve our purpose."

Even with the convincing victory on the Hawks' home ice, the Canucks, to a man, were not about to get carried away. Forward Daniel Sedin even called it "a pretty even game" and sounded like he meant it.

"That's the thing about the playoffs — it's a new game the next game. It doesn't matter if you won 3-2 or 6-1," Daniel Sedin said.

"We need three more. It's not going to come easy. They had more points than us in the regular season. That's a good team. We were lucky on a few goals, but we'll take it and move on."∎

If the idea was to come out and shock Vancouver on Saturday night, then the Blackhawks should consider themselves an unqualified success.

The Canucks had to be stunned at how easy this was. There are remedial shoe-tying classes that are more difficult than their 5-1 victory at the United Center.

In a series that was all but hyped as Bad Blood II: Hate Comes A-Calling, one team looked ready for anything and the other looked ready for a bedtime story.

Thirty-two seconds into the second period, the score was 3-0. It was 5-0 after two periods.

"There's really no excuse to come out flat," Hawks right wing Patrick Kane said.

You'd think the Hawks would have one by now. They have lost the first game of each of their last four playoff series.

The good news is that it's a seven-game series and there is, sources say, a lot of hockey left. But it's hard to explain how they could look so disjointed, so lost, so awful in a Western Conference semifinal that is supposed to be an ode to grit and will.

You saw this kind of head-scratching behavior from the Hawks at times in the Nashville series, so you know they can come back. But it didn't make sitting through Game 1 any easier. It felt like serving a Saturday detention at school.

"We get all those fans out there cheering us on, we should take advantage of the excitement in the building," center John Madden said. "We didn't. We came out flat, and it cost us the first game of the series."

The Canucks scored off rebounds. They scored off a 2-on-1. They scored off excellent passing. The common thread was that Hawks goalie Antti Niemi was under siege for the first two periods, thanks in part to poor team defense. By the third, Cristobal Huet had replaced Niemi.

It might have helped the cause if the Hawks had knocked a Canuck or two off the puck.

"They won the boards," Madden said. "They won the wall battles all the time and the puck battles in front of the net."

Chances were there. Vancouver goalie Roberto Luongo was terrific. The Hawks

apparently aren't rattling around inside his head as much as they might have thought. The guy who cried after the Hawks hit him with a barrage of goals in the playoffs last season was nowhere to be seen Saturday night.

In his place was a dry-eyed goalie who was spectacular at times.

The Hawks had their chances, a good number of them, but Luongo was everywhere. He stopped Brian Campbell as he cut to the net on a power play. He stopped Madden on a 2-on-1. He stopped Kane, who was staring at what looked like a sure goal. And that was just in the first period.

The Hawks had 17 shots in the first and nothing to show for it, other than the notion that if they kept up the pressure, something would have to give. That was the idea, at least. Seems silly in hindsight.

The Hawks are hoping to build off the third period, when Kane scored while they had a two-man advantage. Hey, baby steps, right?

They're up against a lot. Besides reading each other's minds, the Sedin twins surely could see the thought bubbles over the Hawks' heads that said, "Uh-oh." Daniel Sedin kept a play alive behind the net and shoved it to brother Henrik, who beat Niemi from close in.

Above: Patrick Sharp ties the game with his 3rd period goal. Tom Cruze | Sun-Times

period after Antti Niemi yielded two rebounds. Minutes later, Mikael Samuelsson put the Canucks up 2-0, scoring on a wide-open net during a 5-on-3 power play on a nice feed from Henrik Sedin.

But the Hawks recovered, in part, because their defensemen made a concerted effort to get more involved in the offensive zone.

Seabrook ended the Canucks' early momentum by putting in a loose puck from the left circle at 7:40 in the first. The Hawks were outshot 9-1 at that point.

"Getting that goal put in our minds that we can score on this guy," Seabrook said. "We just wanted to get rolling, keep playing hard and do our things and get our opportunities. We had some opportunities last game. We just couldn't bury them. We did a better a job of capitalizing in Game 2."

Niemi continued to show that he can recover after losses as he settled down after the shaky start. The Canucks hit a couple of posts later in the game and maintained some offensive- zone pressure at times. But Niemi (24 saves) came up with several key stops, including a late one on Ryan Kesler.

Luongo (30 saves) did all he could to keep his team in the game. He made key stops on Dustin Byfuglien (who played defense and forward), Marian Hossa and Sharp in the third period.

"It definitely wasn't the start we wanted," Jonathan Toews said. "We had a lot of momentum in the second, and we knew going into the third just down a goal that a lot of the pressure was on them to protect that lead. We got back to playing the way we know we could at that point."■

KRIS VERSTEEG

In the midst of a frustrating night, Kris Versteeg was given another chance to be a hero — the puck on his stick with room to maneuver in the waning moments of regulation in a 2-2 playoff game.

And he blew it.

"I was going to shoot it there, and then four or five bodies went over," Versteeg said. "And then I saw another lane and I kind of double-pumped and lost the puck. I was like, 'Oh my goodness, what the heck did I just do?'"

But just when it looked like it was going to be one of those nights, Versteeg's luck changed in an instant. Brent Seabrook passed to Duncan Keith, who found Versteeg wide open on the left side, with more net than Luongo in front of him.

"I think he was calling pretty loud for that one," Keith said.

Versteeg didn't waste the opportunity, blasting the puck over Luongo's right shoulder with 1:30 to play in regulation for the tie-breaking goal in the Hawks' 4-2 victory over the Canucks that tied their Western Conference playoff series 1-1.

"I was fortunate to get the puck back and I was just trying to shoot it as hard as I could," Versteeg said.

The way things were going for the Blackhawks against Luongo, it was anything but a sure thing.

"You never really know until it goes in," Keith said. "Luongo's a good goalie. He takes up a lot of net. I've seen saves before where you have open nets and the next thing you know he sticks out a leg or pad. Steeger did a good job of bearing down there and burying that one."

Until the game-winner, Versteeg had nothing but frustration to show for his 2010 post-

Above: Kris Versteeg (on knees) scores the go-ahead goal in the 3rd period in Game 2.
Tom Cruze | Sun-Times

season. He came into the game with no goals and two assists and was a minus-3 in seven playoff games. Luongo had stopped him on two great scoring chances in the second period.

"That's what Luongo does best — he frustrates teams by making saves," said Versteeg, who scored 20 goals during the regular season. "It feels good to help this team win. We pride ourselves on four lines and if we're not scoring with all four lines it's going to be tough. We know the third and fourth lines have to step up and help this team out."

Versteeg also assisted on Seabrook's first-

Above: Vancouver defenseman Kevin Bieksa misses a point blank try in the first period. Tom Cruze | Sun-Times

period goal that cut the Canucks' lead to 2-1. He was a plus-3 for the night.

"Those guys came out strong over there," Versteeg said of the Canucks. "It seemed like we came out a little flat and Antti Niemi made some huge saves to keep us in it. It could have been 4-0 pretty easily. You have to give props to him. He made the saves when he had to and it was key."∎

WESTERN CONFERENCE SEMIFINALS

GAME 3:   BLACKHAWKS 5 | CANUCKS 2

The mantras are basically the same, the responses nearly identical.

The Blackhawks and the Vancouver Canucks want to be physically tough to play against while remaining disciplined enough to avoid the penalty box.

It's a fine line to walk, especially when your opponent decides to take it up a notch and you don't respond in kind between the whistles. The Hawks played with that additional edge and evened the Western Conference semifinal series — and then matched and surpassed what the Canucks threw at them Wednesday to take the series lead.

Above: Dustin Byfuglien celebrates a goal with teammates Duncan Keith, left, Patrick Sharp, second from left, and Jonathan Toews during Game 3. AP Photo

It was Dustin Byfuglien who did the most damage, scoring a hat trick and seemingly shoving and yelling at every single Canuck who crossed his path in the Hawks' 5-2 victory in Game 3 at General Motors Place. The Hawks took a 2-1 series lead with Game 4 on Friday.

"Dustin played unbelievable tonight," Marian Hossa said. "He was outmuscling people."

Byfuglien did all his damage in front of the net, scoring on three rebounds yielded by Canucks goalie Roberto Luongo, including two on the power play. But there was more to the victory.

Kris Versteeg and Marian Hossa also scored, and Antti Niemi (31 saves) had another strong game in net for the Hawks, who withstood an early barrage of scoring chances by the Canucks in the first period. The Hawks' penalty kill also stood out, taking care of all four penalties, including Byfuglien's in the third period.

"Every game is different, and we have a ton of respect for the way they play and what they can do out there," defenseman Duncan Keith

Above: Kris Versteeg celebrates after scoring the first goal against Vancouver Canucks goaltender Roberto Luongo in the first period. AP Photo

said. "It's the playoffs, everybody is playing hard and competing."

The series itself was forecasted as a stormy one filled with individual rivalries and a tempestuous history. But the first two games lacked much of the extracurricular rough stuff many had expected — and hoped for — in the series.

It all arrived Wednesday.

There was a lot more jawing, shoving and whacks after plays were blown dead. Between the whistles, there were harder hits and more players laid out on the ice.

Dave Bolland and Daniel Sedin went after each other before a draw during a Vancouver power play and were each assessed roughing penalties — the first roughing calls of the series. Alex Burrows later drew the first unsportsmanlike penalty of the series when he went after defenseman Brian Campbell.

Discipline, though, remained key as the Hawks capitalized with Burrows in the penalty box. Campbell barely reacted as Burrows shoved him into the boards. Three 10-minute misconduct penalties also were called in the final four minutes, including one on Burrows.

The Hawks' biggest response was their ability to score when the Canucks rallied. Jannik Hansen cut the lead to 2-1 9:07 in the second, but Byfuglien responded on the power play.

Burrows made up for his unnecessary penalty by cutting the Hawks' lead to 3-2 with 54 seconds left in the period, but Hossa scored at 7:45 in the third period to seal the victory — off another rebound from Luongo.

"In Game 2, we came out working hard for at least 40 to 50 minutes," Byfuglien said. "We did a very good job this game for full 60."∎

The Blackhawks played with energy and enthusiasm right from the start Wednesday night in a 5-2 victory over the Canucks.

They bothered Vancouver to the point of distraction in Game 3 of the Western Conference semifinals. And they were more physical than at any time during the playoffs.

But ...

It's just that ...

At the risk of sounding like someone who is never satisfied ...

Would the occasional fight be so bad? What we had Wednesday night was two MMA fighters locked in a ground battle.

All the pushing and shoving after the whistle was like watching the drip, drip, drip of a leaky faucet. This is unnatural for hockey players. Somebody do something already.

It's one of the sport's strange quirks that, come playoff time, teams discover the pacifist within.

When the Hawks' Dave Bolland and Vancouver's Daniel Sedin received roughing penalties after a scuffle late in the first period, it was the first time officials had called roughing in this series.

Sequined twirler Johnny Weir might actually survive an NHL playoff game.

Fights are fairly routine during the regular season. They all but disappear in the postseason because penalties can come back to haunt during low-scoring playoff games.

Hawks wing Dustin Byfuglien got a dumb roughing penalty in the third period. If you want to fight, make sure you get the other guy to fight with you. But it's no coincidence that Byfuglien had his best game of the playoffs in this chippiest of games. He plays rough. He played rough on the way to a hat trick Wednesday.

The history between these teams suggests it would behoove the Hawks not to mix it up. In last year's playoffs, Vancouver seemed hell-bent on bullying the Hawks and paid for it with dumb penalties.

And the Hawks frustrated the Canucks again and again Wednesday.

"When we get in their faces, when we get hitting, when we get in there — nobody likes getting hit, right?" Bolland said afterward.

"I don't think anybody likes getting hit against the boards. When you hit, you can do some damage."

This postseason, the Hawks have had to warm up to the idea of checking and hitting people. They have been too docile at times, to the point where they look medicated. They were more into it Wednesday, forcing the action against the Canucks.

Remember kids, violence is never the answer. But this is the NHL, where fighting is allowed, even encouraged, except in the playoffs, when it's shoved in a closet and locked up.

This brings us to Adam Burish and Ben Eager. I've talked a lot about Burish this postseason, about how much the Hawks need him and how silly it has been for coach Joel Quenneville to abandon him at times in favor of more skilled hockey players.

He and Eager add some nastiness to this team. It's as if the Blackhawks remember to start knocking the Canucks off the puck whenever the two are in the lineup.

Given their slow starts in this series, the Hawks should take this a step further. Let Burish in the game early, let him pick out a dance partner and let him get down to the business at hand.

The Hawks haven't always been able to conjure up the proper urgency. This team could use some mass hysteria, some widespread panic, some contagious anger.

Simplistic? Absolutely, but so is hockey. It has been like this forever. Fighting is a bell to which NHL hockey teams answer.

A fight can stop another team from picking on one of your stars. It can fire up your team. It can shift momentum.

And, yes, it can cost you a hockey game, especially in the playoffs.

But sometimes you need to forget what the coach's manual says.

We've heard all about the bad blood between the Hawks and the Canucks, dating to last year's playoffs, but we hadn't seen much of it until Wednesday night.

No one is going to mistake Burish for a heavyweight fighter. He's more of a nuisance than a bully. Eager, on the other hand, is a thumper. Either will do.

Above: Antti Niemi stones Pavol Demitra during the first period of Game 3. AP Photo

★ THREE STARS ★

★ DUSTIN BYFUGLIEN
Without a point in the playoffs coming into the game, Byfuglien scored three goals, two on the power play. He gave the Hawks a 2-0 lead in the first period, a 3-1 lead in the second and was credited with the hat trick after a video review.

★ ANTTI NIEMI
Just as Roberto Luongo did for the Canucks in Game 1, Niemi fended off an early barrage with 16 saves in the first period. That gave the Hawks a chance to take the lead — a critical factor in a road playoff game.

★ MARIAN HOSSA
Hard work finally paid off as Hossa scored a huge goal on a rebound in the third period that gave the Hawks a 4-2 lead with 13:12 left. He also assisted on Kris Versteeg's goal in the first.

At some point in this series, the Hawks are going to need to knock some sense into themselves. They haven't looked like the team with the second-best regular-season record in the Western Conference.

There are times they look like a sleepwalking version of that team.

They were tough and mean Wednesday night, and there's no doubt Vancouver is going to come looking for blood in Game 4 Friday.

The Hawks are not a brawling club. But they aren't shrinking violets either. In addition to being blazingly fast, they're a tough group of kids.

Never mind letting the Canucks know that. They need to remind themselves of it.

We have seen glimpses of the scrappy Hawks of last year's playoffs, a team that played hard from beginning to end. We saw it Wednesday night. We've also seen some people doing a very bad imitation of the team that made it to the conference finals in 2008-09.

Counselors are standing by to figure out why this is happening.

It would be a fascinating study to see if a very talented, very tough team could thrive in the playoffs if it thumbed its nose at conventional wisdom and fought its way to a Stanley Cup.

For now, one fight will do.■

DUNCAN KEITH

It was only a joke. But it spoke volumes as to what type of player Blackhawks defenseman Duncan Keith was about to become.

"We always joked in the minors that there would come a point in his career that he might be able to play the whole game," said Trent Yawney, a former Hawks coach and defenseman who mentored Keith for two years with the Norfolk Admirals of the American Hockey League.

"When he gets tired, everybody else is crawling off the ice."

Keith, 26, leads the Hawks in ice time this season and for the last four years. He also logged the most minutes for Canada, which had several standout defensemen, during its Olympic gold-medal run.

But believe it or not, there was a time when Keith had to fight for ice time. In fact, there were some in the Hawks hierarchy who had their doubts about his potential several years ago.

"The organization at times was up and down with Dunc," said Yawney, now an assistant coach with the San Jose Sharks. "I remember telling former Hawks and current Anaheim Ducks general manager Bob Murray ... to keep an eye on this guy because I don't know how crazy they are about him.

"I said, 'He's not a big guy, but he plays a lot bigger than he is. He's got a lot of attributes that somebody's going to want.'"

Much of the doubt had to do with Keith's size. General manager Stan Bowman said Keith weighed about 151 pounds when the team drafted him with the 54th overall pick in 2002.

"Dunc has been fighting that his whole career because he was a little guy," Bowman said. "I think growing up he's always faced that — 'This kid, he's just too small to play.'"

This is where Keith's off-ice attributes come in. He simply never gave up. Now he is one of the league's best defensemen — and, according to some, the new model for blue-liners in today's NHL, one predicated on speed and skill.

Any doubts are gone.

It's only a commercial, but Keith's "One Goal" spot is becoming a reality. "My goal," Keith says, "is to own the blue line."

Above: Duncan Keith handles the puck. Scott Stewart | Sun-Times

Bowman and Yawney said Keith always had the offensive skills you see now, but he needed to learn the defensive part, which included how to use his stick and quickness.

"Norfolk is where I learned to play pro hockey," said Keith, now a solid 6-1, 196-pounder. "It meant kind of slowing down for me, being in good position, having a good stick and using my strengths, my quickness. It was realizing that being good defensively is how I got into the NHL."

There were times of frustration, especially when others were re-called from Norfolk instead of him, Yawney said. But Keith never lost focus.

"He always wanted to get better right from Day 1 in Norfolk," Yawney said.

"He's got that characteristic that all really good players have, and that's that work ethic, to want to

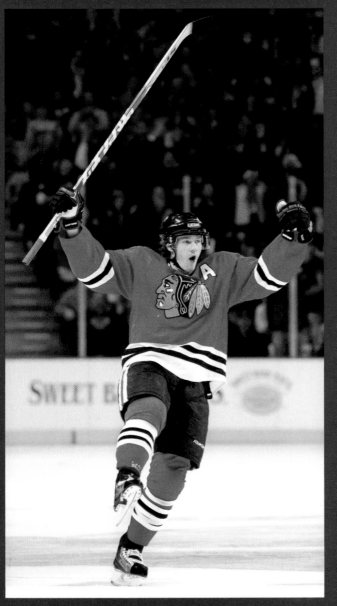

Above: Norris Trophy finalist Duncan Keith celebrates a goal.
Tom Cruze | Sun-Times

Below: Duncan Keith bobble-head. Brian Jackson | Sun-Times

get better and never be satisfied."

Now those really good players consider Keith one of the toughest players to beat.

"He reads the play well," Calgary Flames captain Jarome Iginla said. "He's not the biggest guy or the strongest guy. His speed with a good stick like that, he's tough to get around. He never gives up. He competes very hard."

Combine all that with endurance and fitness levels that prompt Hawks strength coach Paul Goodman to call Keith the "consummate athlete," and what you have is a top-of-the-line player who rarely leaves the ice.

"He's a unique character when it comes to the mental capacity for what he's able to stand," Goodman said. "There is no quit in him."

It's only speculation, but considering Keith as one of the leading candidates for the Norris Trophy, which goes to the best defenseman, isn't far-fetched.

Keith, who signed a 13-year extension in December, has benefitted from playing with Brent Seabrook. But he showed throughout the Olympics that he can be paired with different players at various points of a game and still flourish.

"He has a presence," Versus NHL analyst Brian Engblom said. "Wherever the action is, that's where he is, and he's part of it or has helped create it. ... That's what makes him one of the top defensemen in the game."

Keith also has the numbers. His plus-21 rating may be behind his last two seasons, but he's contributed more offensively. His 59 points trail only Washington Capitals star Mike Green among defensemen, while his 13 goals and 46 assists are career highs.

Used by coach Joel Quenneville in all situations, Keith averages 26 minutes, 39 seconds of ice time -- second-most in the league as of Monday. The impressive thing is that he expends energy associated more with forwards by taking chances offensively and defensively.

"He's a prototypical guy for the way the game is being played now," Engblom said. "He sees the ice and moves at the right time with it.

He moves the puck at the right time, which is more critical in today's game than ever."

Keith also isn't afraid to get physical or drop the gloves when needed. Off the ice, he takes full responsibility for his mistakes and always is willing to face the waiting media, win or lose.

But as far as the Norris Trophy chatter, Keith is not listening to any of it.

"I haven't done anything yet," Keith said, as if he still had something to prove.

"You always want to get better."

THE WORD ON KEITH

"He's a good skater. You got to make sure you don't get in too many races with him. He's going to win those."
— Rick Nash, Columbus Blue Jackets

"With Duncan, it was probably just getting more mature. With years comes maturity and confidence."
— Joe Thornton, San Jose Sharks

"He's a lot better skater than I am, a lot faster, a lot quicker on his skates. I think he's been improving every season."
— Nicklas Lidstrom, Detroit Red Wings, six-time Norris Trophy winner■

Right: Blackhawk defenseman Duncan Keith gets fist bumps from his teammates after scoring.
Tom Cruze | Sun-Times

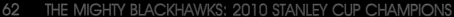

NORRIS TROPHY FINALIST

Duncan Keith never dreamed of becoming a candidate for the Norris Trophy when he signed with the Blackhawks, and it wasn't even foremost on his mind Friday, when he was named one of three finalists for the award honoring the top defenseman in the NHL. Not in the middle of a grind-it-out Stanley Cup playoff series still hanging in the balance.

"That's the beauty of it all, that the team has been playing well and we're in a good battle for the playoffs," Keith said. "That's really what it's all about. It's about your teammates, your team, how the team's doing, and you get a lot of these awards when the team is good."

Keith joined Mike Green of the Washington Capitals and 20-year-old Drew Doughty of the Los Angeles Kings as Norris Trophy finalists.

The Professional Hockey Writers Association votes on the award, with the winner announced June 23 during the NHL Awards show in Las Vegas.

Though Green was runner-up to the Boston Bruins' Zdeno Chara last year, the 26-year-old Keith is considered the favorite by many NHL observers. He would be the Blackhawks' fourth player to win the award and the first since Chris Chelios won his second with the team and third overall in 1996. Hall of Famer Pierre Pilote (1963, 1964, 1965) and Doug Wilson (1982) also won the award with the Hawks.

"Just to be nominated is a huge honor," said Keith, a second-round draft pick (54th overall) by the Hawks in 2002. "You look at other people who've been nominated and other people who have won it, it's a pretty special category, one that I'm proud to be a part of."

Keith had his best offensive year this season, scoring 14 goals with 55 assists for 69 points — the most by a Hawks defenseman since Chelios in 1996 and second-most by an NHL defenseman behind Green (76). Keith also was eighth among defenseman with a plus-21 rating.

But offensive statistics are a fraction of Keith's value to the Hawks. He played in all 82 games. He was second in the NHL in ice-time per game (26:35). He blocked 121 shots. He plays against the opponent's top line more than most defensemen.

Green, 24, is an exceptional player who led defenseman in goals (19), assists (57) and points (76) and was plus-39. But he is considered an offense-first defender who scored 10 of his goals and 35 of his points on the power play.

Keith, who led NHL defenseman in goals and points at even strength, is more consistent and well-rounded. While Green was left off Canada's Olympic team, Doughty and Keith made it because of their better all-around game.

"He Keith does everything great — I was going to say good, but he does everything great," Hawks defenseman Brian Campbell said.

"It's not a case where he's just a power-play guy. He battles against the top lines every night. He puts up numbers. He makes everybody around him better.

"He's definitely my choice for the Norris — and I'm not just saying that because he's my teammate. I've watched him play day-in and day-out and I see what he does. I've seen the other guys and they're special guys. But I don't think anybody in the league brings as much to the table as he does." ■

WESTERN CONFERENCE SEMIFINALS

GAME 4: BLACKHAWKS 7 | CANUCKS 4

The Canucks were hell-bent to prevent Blackhawks winger Dustin Byfuglien from taking over — again.

That meant cross-checking the bruising forward, elbowing him while he tried to put in rebounds and taking whacks at him while he lay on the ice.

After all, as defenseman Brian Campbell put it before the game, Byfuglien is the most hated player in Canada right now.

But all those extra whacks and a handful of other infractions resulted in a parade to the penalty box for the Canucks — and essentially served up a hat trick for Jonathan Toews as the Hawks defeated the reeling Canucks 7-4 in Game 4 on Friday night at General Motors Place.

Toews also assisted on goals by Patrick Sharp (power play) and Brent Seabrook for the Hawks, who now have a commanding 3-1 lead in the best-of-seven Western Conference semifinals. The Hawks can close out the series and advance to the conference finals for the sec-

Above: Chicago Blackhawks Jonathan Toews, second left, celebrates with teammates after scoring a goal. Jonathan Hayward | AP Photo

ond consecutive year with a win in Game 5 on Sunday night at the United Center.

"Jonny had a special night," coach Joel Quenneville said.

Yes, he did. The Hawks' captain tied a franchise record for points (five) in a playoff game and became the first Hawk to score three power-play goals in a playoff game.

Above: Chicago Blackhawks goaltender Antti Niemi keeps his eye on the puck.
Jonathan Hayward | AP Photo

tonight, it doesn't matter who it is — they're going to lose," Canucks coach Alain Vigneault said.

The Canucks said beforehand they planned to crash into Niemi and get into his head — much like the Hawks have set up shop in Luongo's. But the Hawks stood their ground and continued to control the crease — both of them.

Niemi also made big saves to preserve the Hawks' leads, including one on Jannik Hansen when he got behind the defense. Luongo (27 saves) did not.

"Right now, Luongo is the second-best goaltender on the ice," Vigneault said.

Byfuglien did make his presence felt throughout the game, though he did nowhere near the damage he caused in Game 3. In the first period alone, he assisted on Seabrook's goal, drew two cross-checking penalties from defenseman Shane O'Brien and screened Luongo on Toews' first power-play goal. He later endured a few whacks from Alex Burrows after he was knocked to the ice during a scrum in front of Luongo.

The main thing — as the Hawks have maintained all postseason — was that they kept their composure throughout Game 4. An up-and-down first period ended with a 2-2 tie, but then the Hawks scored three power-play goals in the second.

"The No. 1 thing is we focused on our own game," Toews said. "Whether they're reacting negatively to it, it's not really our problem or our priority to worry about it."■

For Toews, though, it was all about the team apitalizing on its chances when it was handed them and not getting sucked into all the extra stuff the Canucks were doing.

"It was nice to get some of those breaks on those chances," Toews said. "We stuck with our game plan, and we know now that nothing they do or whatever is going to take us off."

Tomas Kopecky scored right after a power play expired at 6:49 in the third period, and Dave Bolland added an empty-netter in the final minute for the Hawks. Antti Niemi made 26 saves in the win while Roberto Luongo's teammates did him no favors with eight penalties — many of them needless.

"When any team in the league gives Chicago the number of power plays that we gave them

That sound you just heard was the Blackhawks imposing their will on the Canucks. Or it could have been a referee's whistle.

Whatever it was, the Hawks whacked Vancouver 7-4 Friday night to take a commanding 3-1 lead in their Western Conference semifinal.

The Canucks had eight penalties, leading to four power-play goals faor the Hawks. It was like watching a kid go to pieces at a piano recital.

The series moves back to the United Center for Game 5 Sunday night, and if the Hawks don't revert to the inconsistent team that reared its ugly head at times in these playoffs, it should end there.

This one was impressive. This one was the crusher, and thus it should come as no surprise that it was Jonathan Toews applying the pressure on Vancouver's neck. He had a hat trick by the time the second period was done. He finished with five points.

He's the captain. He's the leader. He's mature beyond his 22 years. And when it came time to put away the Canucks, he was the one who locked them up and threw away the key.

"You always have to have some big performances from guys all over your lineup," he said. "It always seems to be the guy who scores the goals who gets recognized in games like this. But there were guys playing great against some of their top players."

Did we mention he's humble, too?

Nothing against Dustin Byfuglien, who had a hat trick in Game 3, but this was the back-breaker game. This was the one that, going in, the Hawks knew could finish off the Canucks. You look to your best players to come up big in the biggest games. And Toews did.

"You saw the Olympics, that's exactly how he was," said coach Joel Quenneville, referring to Toews' stellar play for Canada in the Vancouver Games.

HELL-OH, VANCOUVER

He was everywhere he was supposed to be Friday night, playing a near perfect game and making life hell for Vancouver.

The Hawks broke it open in the second period with three power-play goals, two by their captain.

It helped that the Canucks' Ryan Kesler shoved the puck from the boards toward his own net and onto Toews' stick for the center's second goal of the night. That occurred 27 seconds into the second period.

The Hawks had four penalties, half of what Vancouver had. The smarter, more disciplined team in this series has been the one that hails from Chicago, and it showed in Game 4.

But you weren't going to hear that from Toews afterward.

"Well, they're going to keep playing the way they play as a team," he said. "They have their own personality, their own character. I guess what you see is what you get."

We saw a Canucks team that had vowed to play rough in Game 4 and ended up playing dumb. It has to be incredibly frustrating to try different approaches in three straight games and to be shot down each time.

Three straight victories for the Hawks is what would be called a trend.

After Friday's loss, Vancouver coach Alain Vigneault was left to pick through the rubble of his team and explain what happened. He said Roberto Luongo was the second-best goalie on the ice, and although that might have been true, the biggest culprit was that his team became unhinged. You could see it as the penalties started to pile up. His Canucks were desperate, and not in a good way.

The young Hawks looked so much more ready for this. Maybe that has something to do with the fact that many of them matured during last year's playoffs.

"It doesn't matter who we're playing or what they're doing, we're sticking to our guns and sticking to what works for us," Toews said. "Doesn't matter what they do to us. Nothing they do is going to take us off our plan."

HUNGRY FOR SUCCESS

Momentum has no shape, but you could see it just as clearly as if it had legs and arms. The Hawks scored 18 seconds into the game.

Can you say hungry? And every time the Canucks answered in the first period, the Blackhawks responded. It was 2-2 after one period, but the momentum arrow was pointed decidedly in the direction of Chicago.

"There are those momentum swings and

Above: Chicago Blackhawk Dustin Byfuglien celebrates a goal on Vancouver Canucks' goaltender Roberto Luongo.
Jonathan Hayward | AP Photo

those emotion swings," Hawks wing Adam Burish said
before Game 4. "In the playoffs, that momentum is so
important. Right now we have it. We've got to try to
find a way to keep it going. After Game 1, they had it.
They probably thought they were going to sweep us."

Burish is one of 11 Hawks who made their playoff
debut last year.

And they're ready for anything now.

"The thing I remember most is just the ups and
downs, just how emotional it is," he said of last season's playoffs. "You lose a game, and you feel like it's
the end of the world. Then you win a game, and you
feel like you can't be beat."

Three victories in a row, two in Vancouver, and the
Canucks in search of their composure. The Hawks
won't be beat Sunday.■

WESTERN CONFERENCE SEMIFINALS

GAME 5:   CANUCKS 4 | BLACKHAWKS 1

It's back to Vancouver for the Blackhawks.

Perhaps there they can relocate their game — the one with the physical style and emotional pace that put them in a commanding position to eliminate the Canucks — because they certainly didn't have it Sunday.

Goalie Roberto Luongo recovered from his back-to-back losses in Vancouver by stopping 29 shots in a 4-1 win for the Canucks

Above: Blackhawks fans look on in shock after the Blackhawks lose 4-1 to Vancouver Canucks.
Scott Stewart | Sun-Times

in Game 5 of the Western Conference semifinals. The Hawks' series lead dropped to 3-2 with Game 6 Tuesday night in Vancouver.

What occurred Sunday was a complete turn of events from how the Hawks prevailed in Games 3 and 4 on the road.

Luongo didn't allow as many rebounds, his much-maligned defensemen cleared loose pucks away, they checked well and, most important, the Canucks stayed out of the penalty box.

As for the Hawks, they didn't get enough traffic in front of Luongo. Dustin Byfuglien, a force in Games 3 and 4, didn't cause nearly as

much havoc, the power play failed to convert and they were the ones who ended up in the penalty box.

"We didn't control the game the way we wanted to," said Hawks captain Jonathan Toews, who scored the Hawks' lone goal at 12:51 in the third period.

"I don't know if we were waiting for someone else to do the job. But we got to all take it upon ourselves to do something, to contribute one way, whether it's scoring a goal or killing off a big penalty."

Before the loss, the Hawks had been 3-0 in elimination games in the last two postseasons.

Above: Hawk left winger Ben Eager and Vancouver defenseman Andrew Alberts lock in a scrum behind the Canuck net late in the 2nd period.
Tom Cruze | Sun-Times

But they didn't come out with the urgency needed to close out the Canucks.

"We weren't good enough tonight," Toews said. "It's as simple as that. ... It's frustrating. It would've been nice to get a big win in our own building, but we knew this team wasn't going to back down."

Canucks defenseman Christian Ehrhoff beat Antti Niemi 59 seconds into the game with a stoppable shot from past the right circle.

Defenseman Kevin Bieksa added two goals, one on a nice setup from Kyle Wellwood that put him in front of Niemi. Alex Burrows added an empty-net goal in the final minute to end any hopes the Hawks may have had.

Vancouver coach Alain Vigneault said the Canucks approached Game 5 with "a one-game mentality." With it, they stayed more composed after committing eight penalties in Game 4 and helped keep the pressure off

Luongo, who struggled with rebound control the last two games.

"We didn't have enough guys in front of the net," winger Kris Versteeg said. "That's it."

Similarly, the Hawks didn't keep things simple, which they did well in the previous two games. Ten Hawks recorded minus ratings.

Versteeg, Byfuglien and Dave Bolland, three of the most effective players in the two wins in Vancouver, were each a minus-2.

"We were looking for more than was out there," Hawks coach Joel Quenneville said. "We were looking for the pretty play rather than simplicity. We didn't have the puck managed very well. We certainly got beat in the faceoff circle. We played smart in our own end but didn't generate anything. We didn't have the necessary traffic in front of the net."■

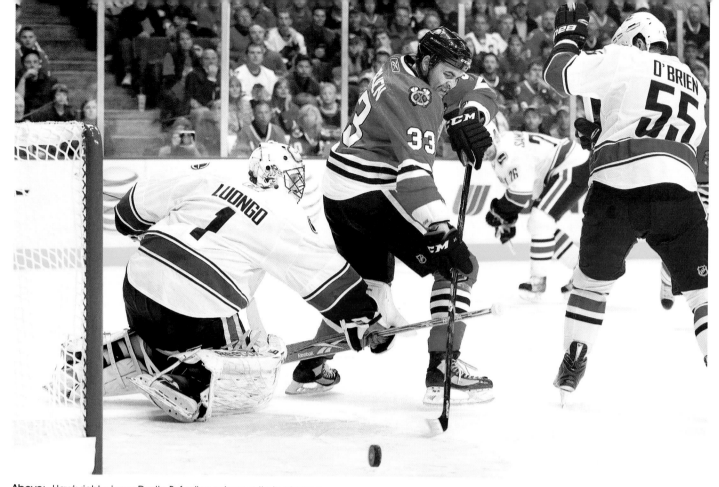

Above: Hawk right winger Dustin Byfuglien misses a tip in chance. Tom Cruze | Sun-Times

The prospect of elimination brought out the best in the Vancouver Canucks.

It's no coincidence they played their best hockey of the Western Conference semifinal series against the Blackhawks in a 4-1 victory Sunday in Game 5 after they finally found a way to chill out.

"Exactly," said defenseman Shane O'Brien, the biggest culprit of the Canucks' emotional meltdowns that had put them in a 3-1 hole heading into Game 5 at the United Center. "Before the game, I'm usually pretty talkative and trying to get the boys going. Today, I just tried to stay focused and take some deep breaths and calm down.

"It's hard for me to do; I like to play with emotion. But you have to control your emotion at this time of year. We learned the hard way in Games 3 and 4. Tonight we were better, and we have to continue to get better at it."

O'Brien, who played less than 10 minutes in Game 4 after being called for two unnecessary penalties that helped pave the way for the

Blackhawks' 7-4 victory, exemplified not only the Canucks' composure, but their grit. O'Brien was bleeding profusely after taking a stick across the face from the Hawks' Dustin Byfuglien.

But he went to the bench, stopped the bleeding and went right back on the ice.

"Obviously, taking two minors in the first period of Game 4, it's unacceptable," O'Brien said. "I was just trying to give 'Big Buff' a hard time, and it ended up costing us. You make mistakes and learn from them and move on. That's what life is all about. It feels good."

The Canucks' victory, which extended the series to Game 6 on Tuesday in Vancouver, was a credit to their defense. Christian Ehrhoff gave the Canucks a 1-0 lead with a slap shot in the first period. Kevin Bieksa scored two goals. And despite losing Sami Salo to an injury at the end of the first period, the Canucks never wavered. And goalie Roberto Luongo stopped 29 of 30 shots.

"The last game, we did some uncharacteristic things," Bieksa said "We're not a team that self-

Above: Antti Niemi can't make the save on the Canucks first goal of the night. Scott Stewart | Sun-Times

★ THREE STARS ★

★ ROBERTO LUONGO

The Canucks goalie rebounded — and so did his rebound control — as he recovered from two poor outings to defeat the Hawks. He made 29 saves and got plenty of help from his defensemen in front of the net.

★ KEVIN BIESKA

The Vancouver defenseman scored twice, including one on the power play at 13:00 in the second period that basically put an end to the Hawks' chances. He also had an assist and a plus-1 rating.

★ CHRISTIAN EHRHOFF

The Vancouver defenseman's goal 59 seconds into the game quieted the boisterous United Center crowd. The solid play of Ehrhoff and others was needed after defenseman Sami Salo left after the first period with an undisclosed injury. Salo was taken to a hospital.

destructs like that. We got frustrated and got caught up in the momentum.

"Tonight, guys were taking punches in the face, sticks to the face. Looie Luongo was still getting run all game, and he sucked it up. That's why we were winners tonight."

"We were calm," Canucks star Daniel Sedin said. "We knew we could play without pressure, and we played our game. This is what we need to bring on home ice, too. We can't get too excited playing in front of our home fans. This is the way we have to play."

At the same time, the Canucks were careful not to make too much of one game.

"We haven't accomplished anything," O'Brien said. "All we did was win one game and get a chance to play more hockey. We're just excited to keep playing."■

TROY BROUWER

Early in the second period of a scoreless Game 6 on Tuesday night against the Vancouver Canucks, Troy Brouwer needed something good to happen almost as badly as the Blackhawks did.

This has been a miserable postseason for the Hawks' third-year forward from Vancouver. A costly turnover in Game 1 against Nashville put him in a playoff funk — no points and a minus-5 in eight games, dwindling ice time and finally three consecutive games as a healthy scratch. And that's just on the ice. All the while, he has been keeping tabs on his ailing father, who's in a rehab facility outside of Vancouver.

So when Brouwer took a perfect pass from Patrick Sharp and knocked the puck past Roberto Luongo to give the Hawks a 1-0 lead two minutes into the second period, it was an even bigger moment than it seemed.

"When I passed him the puck and it went in, I was excited at first that we took the lead," Sharp said, "but then I realized it was Brow and how much that goal meant to him and the rest of the guys. It was a huge lift."

Nobody felt better than Brouwer, with the possible exception of his father watching the game at Laurel Place in nearby Surrey. It was his first playoff point and sparked the Hawks to a 5-1 victory that clinched the Western Conference semifinal series 4-2.

Above: The Chicago Blackhawks celebrate their 5-1 win over the Vancouver Canuck to close out the series, 4-2. AP Photo

Opposite Page: Troy Brouwer celebrates with Patrick Sharp after scoring. AP Photo

★ THREE STARS ★

★ TROY BROUWER
After three games as a healthy scratch, his first goal of the postseason couldn't have been more timely, breaking a scoreless tie off a nice feed from Patrick Sharp two minutes into the second period.

★ KRIS VERSTEEG
The Game 2 hero continued his knack for scoring big goals with a wrist shot that beat goaltender Roberto Luongo in the second period to give the Hawks a 2-0 lead just 36 seconds after Brouwer's goal.

★ ANTTI NIEMI
Can't overstate the importance of his first-period excellence as he stopped all 13 Canucks shots to keep the Hawks in a scoreless game. He made 29 saves overall.

"It felt great," Brouwer said. "My dad's been in a tough situation. He's wanted me to play so badly. For him to watch me play and play in the same city and score my first NHL playoff goal is pretty special."

Brouwer has not used his father's situation as an excuse. But it hasn't been easy.

"Early on," Brouwer said, "it was a little tough. Leaving the rink, calling my mom to see how my dad was doing every day. Now that I know he's made some strides and real good progress, I can focus on hockey. I'm a professional. I can't let those things affect me, but

I was. I'm happy the coaches stuck with me and gave me an opportunity."

That his teammates had his back also helped him pull out of it.

"I told him to stick with it and he's going to score a big goal — even before this series when he wasn't playing," Jonathan Toews said. "He's had nothing but a great attitude.

"That's the great thing about the guys in our locker room. Even when they aren't playing as much, everybody has a great attitude, knowing that when they do get that chance, they can make a difference, and that's what Browsie did for us by getting us on the board first."■

ANTTI NIEMI

So is this it? Antti Niemi or bust? The long Olympic break did little to squelch the debate swirling around the Blackhawks' goalie situation. We know that Niemi will be in goal when the team returns to the ice tonight against the New York Islanders. But has the job become his to lose, or is help on the way?

The Olympic hockey tournament was a reminder about how far an outstanding goalie can take a team. Without Ryan Miller in goal, the United States never would have made it to the gold-medal game.

But here come the Hawks, entering the final stretch of the season with a question mark at the goalie position. It's not an ideal situation.

"We all know the importance of goaltending and what it means to your team and your team's success," coach Joel Quenneville said before the team left Monday for New York. "They're under a lot of scrutiny and a lot of attention. We all know that goalies can win and lose games on their own, and there's a lot of respect in how you view that position."

That said, Quenneville gave both his goalies — Niemi and Cristobal Huet — a vote of confidence.

"We're well aware of our needs and our situation, and we like our group and the progress that we've shown throughout this year," he said. "We're at a point where we're very happy with our goaltending and comfortable with what we have right now."

Whether "right now" means "until the trade deadline Wednesday" remains to be seen. But in the Hawks' defense, it's tough to argue with the job Niemi has done this season. His goals-against average is an excellent 2.16 (the same as the Buffalo Sabres' Miller), and his save percentage is a healthy, if unspectacular, .913.

IS BETTER OPTION AVAILABLE?

But Niemi, who had to battle Corey Crawford just to make the team as Huet's backup this sea-

Above: Hawk goalie Antti Niemi makes a glove save. Tom Cruze | Sun-Times

son, never has faced the intense scrutiny of being the Hawks' main guy. How will he handle the pressure that goes with that job?

"I don't want to think about being No. 1 too much," the quiet Niemi said. "I just want to play as well as I can."

Not that the tight-lipped Hawks have made an official pronouncement about Niemi's status relative to Huet's. No matter what happens next, there will be no coronation for Niemi. Quenneville made a point to say he still wants to give Huet playing time. (As he should, assuming Huet sticks around, because you never know when injury or inefficiency might strike.) But it's clear Niemi has supplanted Huet on the depth chart. Quenneville's decision to go with him for a fifth consecutive game, dating to before the Olympic break, speaks volumes. As does his statement that Niemi "has won, and we don't want to change too much of that."

"He has an opportunity to sustain the net here, and we are going to give him a chance," Quenneville said.

The 26-year-old Finnish rookie has earned a lot of respect for his play. The Hawks like his mental

Hawk goalie Antti Niemi during a second period timeout. Tom Cruze | Sun-Times

toughness, quickness, aggressiveness and confidence. At 6-2 and 210 pounds, he fills the net. Is there a goalie on the market unequivocally better than him?

I suspect general manager Stan Bowman has been asking himself that question a lot lately.

Would the Florida Panthers' Tomas Vokoun or the Montreal Canadiens' Jaroslav Halak, for instance, be a certain improvement? In truth, there isn't a sure thing out there. And even if there was, he would come with no guarantee. Team USA had the best goalie in the Olympics but couldn't beat Canada for the gold.

CUP ROAD TOUGH ON ROOKIES

No matter how much attention we pay to the goalie, he is only part of a winning equation. The Hawks rely on their defense to keep pressure off the goalie, and you can't argue with the success they've had so far. With a 16-point lead on the

Nashville Predators, the Central Division title is a lock. Despite all the hand-wringing around these parts, the Hawks have gotten pretty far with their goalies.

But the postseason is most important, and Niemi never has played in an NHL playoff game. If the Hawks stand pat, they will be tempting fate. Rookie goalies rarely win the Stanley Cup. Since 1971, only three have done it: Ken Dryden and Patrick Roy, two Hall of Famers, and Cam Ward. Of the three, Niemi seems to have the most in common with Ward, who started the 2006 playoffs as a backup for the Carolina Hurricanes.

Do the Hawks dare trust their hoped-for happy ending to a rookie goalie? As the debate swirls around him, the rookie in question seems nonplussed.

"I just want to help the team win," he said. "I try not to think too much. You just want to concentrate on the game."■

Rob Blake (4) of the San Jose Sharks attempts a shot as he is denied by Brent Sopel (5) of the Chicago Blackhawks.

WESTERN CONFERENCE FINALS

GAME 1: BLACKHAWKS 2 | SHARKS 1

The barrage started just over a minute into Game 1 when Sharks winger Devin Setoguchi sent the first shot at Blackhawks goalie Antti Niemi.

The barrage included shots from all angles — the slot, the circles, in close, rebounds, during power plays, on breakouts and redirections.

It was everything from everywhere.

But the Sharks' barrage beat Niemi only once. And in the end, it was Niemi who beat the Sharks, posting a career-best 44 saves in a thrilling 2-1 win Sunday at HP Pavilion in the opening game of the Western Conference finals.

"One of the best, for sure," said the always unassuming Niemi of his performance while at the postgame podium, where media-hounded stars appear after standout performances.

Niemi was the star Sunday. He stood out above the rest, and Game 1 — his first ever against the Sharks — belonged to him.

"He was all right," Hawks captain Jonathan Toews said with a smile. "He's playing great under pressure. ... He was definitely our most valuable player Sunday."

Niemi's performance outshone that of Sharks goalie Evgeni Nabokov, who made 38

Above: San Jose Sharks center Joe Pavelski (8) is unable to score past Chicago Blackhawks goalie Antti Niemi (31). Paul Sakuma | AP Photo

saves and felt plenty of pressure — especially in the third period. But long shots by Patrick Sharp in the second period and Dustin Byfuglien in the third beat Nabokov and gave the Hawks their first 1-0 series lead this post-season.

The Sharks — with some of the NHL's best offensive players in Joe Thornton, Dany Heatley, Patrick Marleau, Dan Boyle and Joe Pavelski — peppered Niemi with 45 shots,

Above: Goaltender Antti Niemi (31) of the Chicago Blackhawks makes a save in the first period. Jed Jacobsohn | Getty Images

including 14 during five power plays. But only one got through — Jason Demers' from the top of the right circle at 11:19 in the first on a power play.

"He had some key saves," coach Joel Quenneville said. "He looked big, took away big parts of the net, dangerous plays, a couple of turnovers, couple not getting it in deep."

Niemi's outing was just another reason that his lack of playoff experience was an overrated concern. He made so many highlight-reel saves Sunday, the tough thing would be determining which was the best.

Was it his absolute thievery against a wide-open Marleau, a 44-goal scorer in the regular season, with his glove in the second period? Or his sprawling glove stop on Ryane Clowe during a Sharks power play later in the same period?

How about one of his stops on Heatley, a two-time 50-goal scorer who had five shots in Game 1? Or his stop on Boyle in the final

minute of regulation during a 6-on-4 Sharks power play?

When asked, Niemi went with his stop on Clowe with 4:12 left in the second period. Niemi yielded a rebound, scrambled to his left and reached out with his glove to stop Clowe's attempt on the goal line. It would have put the Sharks up 2-1.

"I just saw him standing pretty much at the back post with an empty net, and I just wanted to get my hand in the way," Niemi said.

The Hawks clearly fed off the show Niemi was putting on, scoring twice after the Sharks took a 1-0 lead.

"They came out hard and they still scored the first goal, but it could have easily been 2-0 or 3-0," Sharp said. "He made some big saves. ... Nothing surprises me. It's funny we keep talking about him like he's surprising people. If you haven't figured out he's a great goaltender by now, you're not watching the games."■

You don't have to be a hockey expert to know what's going on here.

The best team won.

The Blackhawks aren't the Jordan-era Bulls, but there was something mighty familiar and pretty impressive about the way they reeled in the San Jose Sharks to win 2-1 in Game 1 of the Western Conference finals on Sunday at HP Pavilion.

Outplayed in the first period, particularly in the first 10 minutes, the Blackhawks with their uncanny combination of speed, grit, will and composure, methodically turned this game in their favor. A Brent Seabrook penalty in the second period ignited another Sharks rally. But with Antti Niemi making as many big saves as he has to make, the Hawks withstood the onslaught and regained control in the third period.

SERIES FAR FROM OVER, BUT ...

At this point, you have every right to believe it was only a matter of time before the Blackhawks prevailed. They've won every close game in the postseason: 2-0, 3-0, 5-4 in OT, 5-3, 5-2, 4-2 and now 2-1 against the Sharks to take a 1-0 series lead in the postseason for the first time. Their only losses are 4-1, 4-1, 5-1 and 4-1.

When they're bad, they're bad. But when they're good, they're better than any team left in the Stanley Cup playoffs.

Including the San Jose Sharks.

This series isn't over. It might be far from it. But almost every sign Sunday indicated that the Hawks are in control of this series already. These are still two evenly matched teams. And in hockey as much as any sport, anything can happen. But the Hawks are starting to play like they're as good as they think. It's like watching your teenager become a responsible adult. There might be rough spots ahead, but eventually they'll make it.

Playing in the biggest game of the season in one of the toughest places to play in the NHL, the Blackhawks won their sixth consecutive playoff road game. They had five penalties and zero power plays. In a game that was nearly as physical as it was fast-paced — a style both teams seemed comfortable with — the Hawks had the advantage. The Blackhawks won the matchup battle and made some quick-trigger line changes without drawing a penalty for too many men on the ice. And at the pace it appears this series will be played at, the Hawks' depth is an advantage over the Sharks' superiority with their top two lines.

And it can't be ignored that the Hawks are taking their lead from a 22-year-old captain who is growing up as fast as any player in the postseason.

"Sometimes you have to take a deep breath and not be overwhelmed by the pressure they're throwing at you," Jonathan Toews said. "When things aren't going your way, you can't get too depressed. There's always a way out of it."

Only when the Blackhawks lost their precious "puck possession" did they falter in this game. After being outshot 13-8 in the first period, they outshot the Sharks 14-6 in the first 14 minutes

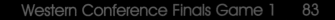

(2nd L) Dustin Byfuglien (33) of the Chicago Blackhawks reacts with teammates after his third period goal.

of the second. After Seabrook's holding penalty, the Sharks outshot the Hawks 12-0 through the rest of the second period. But it wouldn't be long before the Hawks regained control.

TOEWS CALLS IT 'WORK ETHIC'
How do they do it?

"Just work ethic," Toews said. "As games go along, we have four lines that can skate and four lines that can handle the puck.

Nobody's getting worn down that way. We can all play physical through three periods.

"That's what you saw tonight. We stuck with it. The more chances, the more you have the puck, the better the chances are that you're going to score and win the game."

There's still a long way to go. The Blackhawks have to brace themselves for a likely Sharks onslaught in Game 2, and the daunting challenge of winning at home awaits. But even though most playoff victories are a singular event, this one seemed to say much more: This series is the Hawks' to lose.■

★ THREE STARS ★

★ ANTTI NIEMI
The Hawks goalie introduced himself to the Sharks in spectacular fashion. In his first career start vs. San Jose, Niemi made a career-high 44 saves, including several highlight-reel stops. Niemi faced 45 shots, the most since he turned away 35 of 38 in a win over Detroit on Jan. 17.

★ EVGENI NABOKOV
The Sharks goalie may have lost the duel vs. Niemi, but he kept his team in the game by turning away several good chances by the Hawks, who dominated at times. Nabokov finished with 38 saves and did a good job of eliminating second and third opportunities by pouncing on loose pucks in front of his net.

★ DUSTIN BYFUGLIEN
The Hawks winger had a couple scoring chances prevented by a concerted Sharks effort to raise his stick and get better position.

"They do a very good job at it," said Byfuglien, who scored the winner from the top of the slot at 13:15 in the third period after Jonathan Toews won a faceoff and Patrick Kane fed him the puck.

ANTTI NIEMI

Just a reminder: Antti Niemi is a goalie, not a god.

"He's no different than most goalies," San Jose Sharks defenseman Dan Boyle said Monday. "He made some big saves last game. I saw some of the replays of the saves he made and they were big. But I don't think it's anything we need to discuss more."

Boyle's exasperation underscored the frustration of each of the Blackhawks' postseason opponents. You see Niemi allow four goals in a bad loss and you know he's vulnerable. Then he stones you with 44 saves, you end up losing a game you think you should have won and the question is whether you can "'solve" Niemi to avoid a 2-0 deficit in the Western Conference finals.

"It's the same thing, man," Boyle said. "Every goalie. I'm repeating myself. It's traffic. It's rebound goals. We had a bunch of pucks laying around — Ryane Clowe, Joe Pavelski — one of those pucks go in, it's a different story.

"He's no different than the way we treat Marty Brodeur — with the exception of the way goalies handle the puck. But whether it's Brodeur, Niemi ... it's traffic, shots at the net, rebounds. It's the same thing."

But as Game 2 of the series beckons at 9 tonight (Versus, 560-AM) at HP Pavilion, it's the Hawks who have to remember that, as hot as Niemi was in their 2-1 victory over the Sharks on Sunday, he is still a rookie goaltender — and unlikely to fare as well against another 45-shot onslaught.

"You don't want to go to the well too many times," forward Patrick Sharp said. "He made huge saves that easily could have been in the back of the net. We know he'll rise to the challenge, but eliminating chances is key for us."

Above: Chicago Blackhawks right wing Dustin Byfuglien (33) celebrates next to San Jose Sharks center Patrick Marleau (12) after scoring. Paul Sakuma | AP Photo

"We have to block more shots in front of him," forward Marian Hossa said. "He was unbelievable Sunday. We just have to make sure we make his job a little easier."

Niemi has been a revelation in the playoffs. But he hasn't been perfect. His two shutouts against the Nashville Predators in the first round were followed by four-goal games.

Only in Games 2 and 3 against the Vancouver Canucks, which the Hawks won 4-2 and 5-2, has he put together back-to-back solid games in a series. And in those games he faced 26 and 23 shots, nowhere near the test he aced in Game 1 against the Sharks.

The Hawks know they have to keep the heat off Niemi. They can start by cutting down on penalties, which gave the Sharks five power plays in Game 1. San Jose scored on one, but even after a successful penalty kill in the second period, the Sharks sustained the momentum for a 12-0 edge in shots in the final 5:59 of the second period.

Another focus is drawing a penalty or two on the Sharks and putting them back on their heels. The Sharks had zero penalties in Game 1 — only the second time in 432 NHL playoff games since the lockout a team was not penalized in a playoff game.

But that could still be problematic for the Hawks. While the Sharks' having no penalties was a rarity, it was not a fluke. They have had just 38 penalty-kill situations in the postseason, the fewest of the conference finalists. The Hawks with 58 have the next fewest.

Four of the Hawks' nine postseason victories have come without a power-play goal. But in three of those, Niemi has come up big. With the Sharks expected to be at their best to avoid a 2-0 hole at home, leaning on Niemi again could be a mistake.

"It's something we have to be ready for," defenseman Duncan Keith said. "We can't rely upon Antti to make those saves game after game." ▪

GAME 2:   BLACKHAWKS 4 | SHARKS 2

Maybe coach Joel Quenneville and general manager Stan Bowman should seriously consider putting the Blackhawks in a hotel before all games, home and away.

The Marriott? The Hilton? The Ritz? Anywhere would do if it helps the Hawks hold onto that winning edge they have on the road.

The Hawks matched the San Jose Sharks' sense of urgency and desperation Tuesday in Game 2 of the Western Conference finals — and eventually surpassed it for a 4-2 win at HP Pavilion.

The Hawks' best players were exactly that as Jonathan Toews had a power-play goal and an assist and Patrick Kane and Duncan Keith each recorded two assists. Toews extended in his point streak to a career-high 11 games, which tied a franchise record held by Stan Mikita.

Andrew Ladd, Dustin Byfuglien and Troy Brouwer also scored as the Hawks made a loud statement by taking a 2-0 series lead with two wins in San Jose, one of the NHL's toughest places to play on the road.

It was the Hawks' seventh consecutive win on the road this postseason, which ties a league record. The Hawks are 7-1 away from the United Center, site of Game 3 on Friday night.

"It's just being focused more than any-

Above: Chicago Blackhawks center Jonathan Toews (19) celebrates next to San Jose Sharks goalie Evgeni Nabokov (20), after right wing Dustin Byfuglien scores. Paul Sakuma | AP Photo

thing," Keith said of the road success. "It's mentally being focused and understanding what we have to do and not deviating from that. For whatever reason, when we're at home — we haven't been at home in a long time mind you — but I think before when we were at home we were guilty of being a little too cute with the puck and a little fancy. When

Above: Chicago Blackhawks goalie Antti Niemi (31) blocks a shot by a San Jose Sharks player. Paul Sakuma | AP Photo

we're on the road, the guys are making the simple plays. We're going to do that when we go home now."

The simple plays — as the Hawks have maintained all postseason — include finishing their checks, not making the risky plays and getting traffic in front the net. It also involves being patient and sticking to their puck-possession game.

The Hawks did that Tuesday much better than they did in Game 1 as the number of shots dramatically decreased for both teams. Goalie Antti Niemi (25 saves) was brilliant again, especially in the first period, when the Sharks outshot the Hawks 10-3 seemingly in a matter of minutes before the Hawks recovered.

"What a way to start the series," center Patrick Sharp said. "To win two games here is huge going forward. I thought we got better and better as the game went on again. They came out with a huge push to start the game,

but we did the little things, winning faceoffs, blocking shots, and our power play got another big goal for us."

Ladd, Byfuglien and Toews gave the Hawks a 3-0 lead before the Sharks regained some life on Patrick Marleau's power-play goal at 11:08 of the second period when Dave Bolland, one of the Hawks' best penalty-killers, was in the box.

The Sharks had their surges but couldn't break through.

Frustrations appeared to boil over in the third. Bolland was the center of it as Thornton, who is a minus-10 in the playoffs, slashed him on a faceoff.

"We played such a good game when we were leading, we didn't let them shoot at all," Niemi said. "I think they maybe got a little frustrated, especially at the end when they were taking penalties."

Losing two games in a row at home can do that to a team.■

I don't mean to rain on your championship parade, but does the Blackhawks' dismantling of the San Jose Sharks in the first two games of the Western Conference finals strike you as too easy?

These are the Hawks, and this is Chicago. Isn't there at least supposed to be loss of limb involved?

Surely you remember the Hawks of the previous two playoff series.

They were a team that could be counted on to make life as hard on itself as on opponents, a team that alternately amazed and bewildered. How the Hawks played depended on the day, the Dow Jones Industrial Average, the relative intensity of coach Joel Quenneville's glower, ice conditions, biorhythms, Patrick Kane's mullet. Who knew why they'd be great one night and asleep another?

So now this same up-and-down team is indicating it has no intention of descending from the mountaintop. Wonderful. Love the attitude.

Just this once, it would be nice if MapQuest could suggest an easy route for the Hawks.

But ... really? It's going to be this simple?

That's hard to imagine, given the collective experience of the city. It's not as though there's a long history of teams cooperating with paying customers' dreams. Most people here have trust issues encoded in their DNA.

Two road victories against the team that had the best record in the conference, and now some of you are trying to figure out if you can afford a trip to Philadelphia for the Stanley Cup finals.

If you look up, there's a decent chance you'll see a grand piano hurtling down toward you.

Team must play better at home.

This is a team that wasn't sure about its goalie going into the playoffs. You remember Antti Niemi. He's the guy who took you by the hand on a crisis of confidence at the start of the playoffs.

Now you like his Hall of Fame chances. Now you're thinking of taking Finnish as a Second Language.

Again, wonderful. Nice to see those sou-

venir playoff towels all aflutter at the United Center. But have you noticed the Hawks haven't played particularly well at home in the postseason?

I know: Nobody wants to hear it. Nobody wants a naysayer even whispering nay. You would prefer to think about happy things, such as drowning out the anthem singer.

But isn't the wise thing — the time-honored Chicago thing — to brace yourself for inevitable hardship? That way, when it comes, it won't come as such a shock.

Unless, of course, hardship never comes.

Nah, couldn't be. It has been 18 years since the Hawks were in the Stanley Cup finals and almost 50 years since they won the title.

And now we're supposed to believe a toothless Sharks team can't eat solids?

Let's agree on this: In Game 3 on Friday, the Hawks have to get over whatever it is that has bothered them at home in the postseason. They're 3-3 at the United Center. They have been phenomenal away from home. They tied an NHL playoff record with their seventh consecutive road victory Tuesday.

There are lots of things going the Hawks' way, besides Niemi's Gumby act. They have

Above: Scott Nichol (21) of the San Jose Sharks shoots a wrap-around on goaltender Antti Niemi (31) of the Chicago Blackhawks. Jed Jacobsohn | Getty Images

Opposite Page: Duncan Keith (2) of the Chicago Blackhawks shoots the puck. Ezra Shaw | Getty Images

★ THREE STARS ★

★ DUNCAN KEITH
The Norris Trophy finalist played a critical role as the Hawks withstood the Sharks' early assault. He then assisted on Andrew Ladd's first-period goal that gave the Hawks a 1-0 lead and fired a slap shot that Jonathan Toews deflected in for a 3-0 lead in the second period.

★ JONATHAN TOEWS
The dependable captain continues to make a living by being in the right place at the right time. He assisted on Dustin Byfuglien's second-period goal that gave the Hawks a 2-0 lead, then scored his seventh goal of the postseason on a deflection in front of the Sharks' net for a 3-0 lead.

★ ANTTI NIEMI
He didn't face the 45-shot barrage he did in Game 1, but he probably could have the way he played again. He stymied the Sharks from the outset, stopping 10 shots early. That allowed the Hawks to score the first goal.

momentum. They have pesky Dave Bolland, who could cause the guards at Buckingham Palace to lose their composure.

One game at a time. They have four legitimate lines, and Quenneville has been able to mix-and-match with success throughout the playoffs. When the players say they're comfortable on any line, they mean it. Recall that in the series against the Nashville Predators, Bryan Bickell was on a line with Kane and Jonathan Toews. The Hawks won all three of those games. Bickell has played a total of 23 NHL games in three seasons.

After their 4-2 victory Tuesday, some of the Hawks were talking about the importance of taking it one game at a time. For once, the cliché was absolutely dead-on. Brian Campbell said they couldn't get too far ahead of themselves. Again, dead-on.

"We just haven't taken anything for granted," Toews told reporters.

"We go into these games just putting all the pressure on the other team. We go out there and play loose, play hard, simple, the right way."

This is a very good sign — a team that looks in the mirror and acknowledges the presence of Jekyll and Hyde.

"I think the guys have been really focused as we progressed here — not being satisfied going into games or, after games, not being too excited or too high," Quenneville said.

Not only did the Hawks win Game 1 of a series for the first time in five tries, they dominated the Sharks in Game 2. It's all going so smoothly. Too smoothly.

Two road victories to open the conference finals.

This is easy.

Too easy.

Does anyone else see that blinking "Danger Ahead" sign? I didn't think so.■

JONATHAN TOEWS

Above: Jonathan Toews scores as Vancouver Canucks goalie Roberto Luongo can't make the save. Scott Stewart | Sun-Times

From the mouth of any other 21-year-old hockey player, Jonathan Toews' optimism would have rung hollow. The Blackhawks had just been outplayed by the Nashville Predators in a 4-1 loss that put his team in a hole that seemed much larger than two games to one.

"The good thing is we didn't play our best game," Toews said. "If we would have executed the way we wanted to and still lost 4-1, then we would be in trouble. But we have so many different ways we can improve. There's no reason to get depressed about it."

But besides looking at the bright side, Toews also challenged himself and his team to do something about it.

"We have to find a way to produce," he said. "It starts with guys like myself. We all have to look at ourselves as individuals and find that little extra we can bring."

It is unlikely coincidental that in the 17 days since Toews spoke those words, the Hawks have gone from potential first-round upset victim to serious Stanley Cup contender. They've won six of seven games — including four straight on the road — to oust the Predators and take a 3-1 lead on the Vancouver Canucks in the Western Conference semifinals.

And Toews, befitting his role as captain, is leading the way. After the bad loss to the Predators, Toews had one point and was minus-3 for the postseason. In the seven games since then, he has five

Hawk captain Jonathan Toews readies himself for a faceoff. Tom Cruze | Sun-Times

goals and 12 assists for 17 points and is plus-6.

Toews, who turned 22 on April 29, has totaled 13 points in the Hawks' last four road games, capped by a three-goal, five-point night in the 7-4 victory Friday. His 18 points in 10 playoff games lead the league.

"It seems like we're always talking about Jonny and how well he's playing, and how he always steps up in the big games," Patrick Sharp said. "It's not a surprise to me or any of my teammates that he always comes through. That's why he's our leader. He's great in all areas — from faceoffs to putting the puck in the net to keeping it out."

When he's surrounded by good players, Toews is tough to beat. He led Team Canada's gold-medal-winning Olympic team with eight points. He only scored one goal, but it was a big one — the first in the gold-medal game against the United States.

"Jonny's a special player," Hawks coach Joel Quenneville said. "He epitomizes what leadership is all about. When the stakes get higher, he seems to rise to the occasion. He seems to relish the environment."

Those intangibles enhance Toews' all-around skills. When he's hot, he always seems to be in the right place at the right time.

"Some nights you're not going to play your best, and everything goes in for you," Toews said. "Obviously last night was one of those nights where you're around the net and everything seems to find you, and you get lucky.

"You work hard over an extended amount of games, and sometimes you don't get those breaks and it gets frustrating. But it's playoff hockey. You have to stick with it, and eventually you're going to cash in and help your team in a big way like that. That's what I've been trying to do."∎

Chicago Blackhawk (33) Dustin Byfuglien
shoots and scores the game winner goal
over the Sharks. Scott Stewart | Sun-Times

Western Conference Finals Game 3 '93

WESTERN CONFERENCE FINALS

GAME 3: SHARKS 2 | BLACKHAWKS 3 (OT)

The legend of Big Buff continues to grow. The "little rat" continues to make a decisive impact. And the Blackhawks are one win away from reaching the Stanley Cup finals for the first time since 1992.

Dave Bolland's behind-the-net pass to a wide-open Dustin Byfuglien in front of an unsuspecting Evgeni Nabokov resulted in the game-winning goal in the Hawks' 3-2 overtime victory against the San Jose Sharks in Game 3 of the Western Conference finals

Above: Dustin Byfuglien celebrates after scoring the winning goal in overtime to beat the Sharks 3-2.
John J. Kim | Sun-Times

Friday night at the United Center. The Hawks have a 3-0 series lead.

"I don't know how to say it, but that's a pretty darn good feeling," Kris Versteeg said of the game-winner. "It was a big night by a lot of guys."

None bigger than Bolland, who made up for his three penalties with a third-period goal and the setup for Byfuglien, who continues to be in the right place at the right time this

postseason.

"[Byfuglien] just keeps scoring big goals and making big plays — none bigger than the one he had tonight," winger Patrick Sharp said. "[Bolland] had a nice goal there, too."

Sharp scored on the power play and Jonathan Toews had two assists for the Hawks, who got another shutdown effort from their penalty kill. Toews extended his points streak to 12 games, setting a franchise record

Above: Dustin Byfuglien (33) shoots and scores the game winner over the Sharks. Scott Stewart | Sun-Times

by surpassing Stan Mikita's 11-game mark.

Antti Niemi stood out again in net, stopping 44 of 46 shots and tying his career high in saves that he set in Game 1 of the series. He was particularly strong in the third period - despite Patrick Marleau's game-tying goal with 4:23 left - as the Sharks outshot the Hawks 18-6 in the third and 41-27 through three periods.

The desperation was clear on the Sharks' part.

"[Niemi is] nice to have back there, that's for sure," veteran center John Madden said.

Penalties were a problem for the Hawks. Six were called on them, including three in the third period. That was the main reason for the Sharks' big shot differential.

Nabokov (35 saves) appeared to battle shots at times but was strong in overtime, stopping a redirection by Andrew Ladd and Patrick Kane in close.

In the end, a defensive breakdown led to Nabokov's demise and the Hawks being one win away from advancing.

"Every game is the biggest game in the play-offs — next game is always the biggest," Sharp said. "We're not even thinking about advancing. We're thinking about that next game and keeping these guys off the score-board."

The Hawks have kept things in perspective. They have a patent on the one-game-at-a-time mentality. But it's hard not to get excited. It's hard not to look ahead when all that's needed is one more nail in the Sharks' coffin.

"We can't give that team any life and head back to their building," Madden said. "We're going to enjoy this win. But we're going to talk about [Sunday today] and refocus and get things going again."∎

As it turns out, you can go home again and collect hotel reward points at the same time. Pretty sweet deal.

The Blackhawks, a team that has struggled to explain why it has struggled at the United Center in the playoffs, won't have to, at least for a day.

Dustin Byfuglien scored a goal in overtime to give the Hawks a 3-2 victory over San Jose on Friday night.

They have a 3-0 lead in the Western Conference finals, and given their struggles at the UC in these playoffs, no one should be silly enough to guarantee they'll wrap up the series Sunday at home.

It's tempting, but don't do it.

Instead, enjoy the fact that the Hawks might have stumbled on a way to get over their problems at home: pretend they're somewhere else.

Having played so well on the road in the playoffs, the Hawks spent Friday afternoon in an area hotel, hoping to simulate a road trip.

Maybe they need to be sequestered like a jury all the time. They can enjoy overpriced cashews from the room mini-bar, a free USA Today in the morning and a knock from housekeeping even when the "Do Not Disturb" sign is hanging from the doorknob.

""I think it helped," forward Patrick Sharp said of the brief hotel stay. "We played well. There was no issue with the way we came out on home ice. I don't think that's an issue anymore.

"We played [Friday night] the way we did for the last two years just about every game at home, and really used the crowd to our advantage. I'm sure Madison [Street] is rocking now. It's going to be fun coming out for the anthem for Game 4."

Ah, Game 4 — also known as One Game from the Stanley Cup Finals. But who's counting?

It was Dave Bolland's pass from behind the net that gave Byfuglien a clear shot from the slot. The goal with 7 minutes, 36 seconds left in overtime set off a celebration inside the stadium and around the city.

Oh, what a relief it was

It was Bolland's goal that had given the Hawks a 2-1 lead with about five minutes left

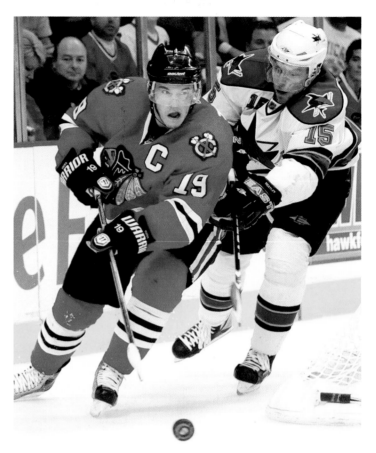

Above: Jonathan Toews (19) maneuvers the puck toward the Sharks goal in the first period. John J. Kim | Sun-Times

in the third period. Jonathan Toews had blocked a shot and the puck skittered ahead to Bolland, who skated in for a breakaway goal to give the Hawks the lead.

Let's just agree that Toews is everywhere the puck is when it matters, OK? Life will be a lot easier if we all understand that.

With Bolland's goal, there was a decided feeling of relief inside the UC, as if something had been settled with it — if not the game, then at least the idea that the Hawks had overcome their silly home-ice problem.

Except they hadn't, not yet. The Sharks' Patrick Marleau scored off a scramble in front of goalie Antti Niemi a few moments later, and just like that, the scored was 2-2. Uh-oh would soon become OT.

The Hawks said they weren't worried.

"We've been good all year at regrouping after a team comes back late or being in tough situations," forward Andrew Ladd said. "I thought we did that again [Friday night]. I thought we were really strong in overtime."

Early on, it seemed like the same old Hawks at home.

Above: Antti Niemi blocks a shot on goal in the third period. John J. Kim | Sun-Times

There was a stretch in the first period when all the doubts crept back in about their ability to play with passion at home. They reverted to their unfortunate habit of not getting to the puck first. Because of it and because they went a long time without a quality scoring opportunity, a heaviness settled over the crowd. It felt like a game with all of the urgency of a January matchup against Buffalo.

And that was the big fear going into this game, that the Hawks' inability to scare up some emotion at home would rear its sleepy head again.

They were 3-3 at the UC going into Friday's game. They had won seven straight playoff road games.

But they found themselves in Game 3, quickly and just in time.

"Both teams played like it was already Game 7," Toews said.

Hard to resist temptations

The Hawks had talked about the temptation of trying to put on too good a show for the home fans with fancy stickhandling. But outside of Patrick Kane, nobody else fit that profile and generally, Kane's game is based on his slickness with the puck, home and away.

Maybe they have a tendency to get too jacked up, starting with the roar during the national anthem. Whatever the problem was, it had become much bigger than it should have been. Maybe it's over now.

It's easy to lose sight of the fact that the Sharks are a very good team. The Hawks won the first two games of this series in San Jose, and it was naïve to think the Sharks were going to lie down on the ice and freeze to death. They were the No. 1 seed in the conference for a reason.

"Every game's been harder and harder to play in," Sharp said. "We expect that with Game 4."

At least they'll be at home. Who knew that was a positive?■

Above: An NHL Official meets with Chicago Blackhawk Captain Jonathian Toews (19) at center ice before the official ceremony of the Clarence Campball Trophy.   Scott Stewart | Sun-Times

Blackhawks captain Jonathan Toews certainly saw the shiny Clarence S. Campbell Bowl sitting atop a table in the middle of the United Center ice.

But he stopped about a foot short of the trophy, which is awarded to the Western Conference champion.

It's not that he didn't want to touch it or that he strictly abides by all league superstitions. It just wasn't the trophy he wants to hoist. It wasn't the Stanley Cup.

But Toews and the Hawks will get their chance soon enough to hoist what they covet after completing a sweep of the San Jose Sharks in the conference finals with a 4-2 victory Sunday.

With the win, the Hawks booked their first trip to the Stanley Cup finals since 1992. They await the winner of the Eastern Conference finals between the Philadelphia Flyers and Montreal Canadiens.

"It's not what we want to win," Toews said. "They gave us hats tonight, so we'll go home with those and we'll be happy about that. We're after something bigger and better.

"We worked so hard to get here. It's been a long year. There was so much going on and off the ice. Everything that was said and the story lines and all that stuff we've tried our best to ignore. We have a great opportunity. We'll be very excited about it, and we'll go work for it. That's what we're here for."

The Toews-Patrick Kane-Dustin Byfuglien combination delivered the game-winner during a power play at 14:05 of the third period as the Hawks overcame a 2-0 deficit.

Above: Dave Bolland (36) and teammates celebrate his goal that sailed over San Jose Sharks goaltender Evgeni Nabokov. This tied the game at 2-2. Scott Stewart | Sun-Times

Byfuglien was parked in front of Sharks goalie Evgeni Nabokov when Kane set him up. Toews also assisted to extend his team-record points streak to 13 playoff games.

It highlighted another comeback in the series by the Hawks, who overcame the loss of Andrew Ladd (undisclosed injury) after four shifts and Duncan Keith for a stretch of the second period after taking a puck in the mouth.

"It's pretty surreal right now to realize how far this team has come in such a short time," an out-of-breath Kane said. "This is nice and all, but we're not finished yet."

Antti Niemi, a star in all four games of the series, made 16 saves as the Hawks held the Sharks to by far their lowest shot total of the series. The Sharks, so desperate early in the game, wore down in the end as the Hawks held them to three shots in the third period.

Brent Seabrook and Dave Bolland scored in the second to swing the momentum in the

Hawks' favor. Seabrook's goal at 13:15 restored the pandemonium feel in the United Center after it was reviewed for several minutes.

Kris Versteeg iced the victory with an empty-netter with 42 seconds left. Patrick Marleau (short-handed) and Logan Couture scored for the Sharks.

"It's unbelievable [sweeping the Sharks]," Kane said. "So many guys have stepped up. Every game was a new challenge for us. It looked like things weren't going to go our way today, and we still stepped up and got the win. It's a really cool feeling right now."

It will be even cooler competing for the Cup, which the Hawks haven't touched since 1961.

"No one ever dreams of getting to the Stanley Cup, to be honest with you," Kane said. "You dream of winning the Stanley Cup."▪

This didn't come out of nowhere, out of thin air or out of the blue. The Blackhawks had been building up to what happened Sunday afternoon for two years.

But when the moment came, when Kris Versteeg swept the puck into an empty net and the fans at the United Center started doo-doo-doo-dooing along with that crazy, wonderful, joyous song "Chelsea Dagger," it felt as sudden as a heart attack. You know, in a good way.

The Hawks still can thrill, maybe to excess at times, but good Lord can they thrill, all the way to the Stanley Cup finals. Their 4-2 victory over the Sharks completed a four-game sweep, which sounds dominant - perhaps because it is. Not easy, but dominant.

For the first time in 18 years, the Hawks will play for a championship named after Lord Stanley.

And they should win it for the first time in almost half a century.

"Last year we were in [the Western Conference finals], but I don't know if we knew we were going to win that round," Hawks winger Patrick Kane said. "We didn't have the confidence.

"This year, it's almost like we feel that we shouldn't lose a game, to be honest with you. It's not cocky. That's just our attitude. We just feel like we have such a good team."

Depth hard to beat

They should because they do. They likely will play Philadelphia, which has a 3-1 series lead over Montreal in the Eastern Conference finals. As hot as the Flyers are, they are not the team the Hawks are.

Anyone who saw the Hawks take apart the Sharks on Sunday took in an impressive amalgam of talent and grit.

There was Kane, Jonathan Toews and Dustin Byfuglien, who scored the game-winner on a power play in the third period.

There was Brian Campbell, Patrick Sharp, Brent Seabrook, Marian Hossa and Dave Bolland, who floated in a wrist shot to tie the game 2-2 in the second.

Above: No.33 Dustin Byfuglien starts to celebrate his tie-breaking goal. 3-2 Hawks. Scott Stewart | Sun-Times

There was goalie Antti Niemi, the question mark before the playoffs who has turned into an exclamation mark.

And there was Duncan Keith, which rhymes with "teeth," of which the defenseman was missing seven after taking a puck to the mouth in the second period. He came back to play soon after, of course. He's a hockey player, and teeth are sort of like fingernail clippings.

When you add experience to the equation, it's hard to see what would get in the Hawks' way to a title. What we saw Sunday was the culmination of two years of living and learning. The Hawks reached the conference finals last year but received an education in professionalism from the Red Wings.

"Last year we celebrated victories too much and looked ahead too much," Campbell said. "Now we're focused on each individual effort."

So on Sunday, there wasn't the kind of mad, champagne-fueled locker-room celebration you see when a major-league baseball team wins a wild-card playoff berth. There was an understated room of people who agree there's more work to do.

"I haven't won anything yet," Campbell said, shrugging. "Nobody else in this locker room has. I don't know why there would be a celebration."

Well, there was the fact that the Hawks avoided going back to San Jose for Game 5. That was worth celebrating. So was how they won Sunday. They came back to grab their second consecutive game at the United Center, which hasn't been kind to them in the playoffs.

San Jose was the early aggressor, taking a 2-0 lead. In one 16-minute span, the Hawks had one shot on net. What's the hockey term for "not good"?

They decided to go with what brought them here, which is speed. They forced the pace, and the Sharks had trouble keeping up.

It's been awhile

Not long after Byfuglien beat Sharks goalie Evgeni Nabokov to give the Hawks a 3-2 lead, the UC scoreboard showed Bobby Hull, Stan Mikita and Tony Esposito standing together. OK, we got the message: It's been a long time. Hull and Mikita were on the 1961 team that won the Stanley Cup.

After Versteeg scored the goal that put the game out of reach with 42 seconds left, fans started tossing souvenir red towels onto the ice. Workers with shovels collected them. Brooms would have worked better.

And all that time, The Fratellis' "Chelsea Dagger" throbbed throughout the building. It's the song the Hawks play after their goals, and, man, did it rock Sunday.

"I hear that song every time my son's phone rings," center John Madden said. "That's what he has on his ringer. I just giggle. He thinks it's great. Everybody does."

Everybody but the good people of Nashville, Vancouver and now San Jose. Suggestion for the Flyers or the Canadiens: earplugs.

Whether the Hawks play Philadelphia or Montreal, they are going to be the favorite to win the Stanley Cup. Heavy favorites. As they should be.

It will be a new feeling for Madden, who won a Cup with the New Jersey Devils in 2003.

"We kind of hid under the radar, all the way to the end," he said. "We didn't even have a parade in Jersey. It was in a parking lot. We walked on stage and walked off."

If the Hawks win the Cup, there will be parades, parties, maybe even a symposium or two to acknowledge the feat. Championships have not been known to grow on trees here.

But a celebration beforehand? No. Not now, not yet. ∎

COACH JOEL QUENNEVILLE

Above: Hawks coach Joel Quenneville works the referees from the bench. Tom Cruze | Sun-Times

I t's a simple game played as practice comes to an end. But it shows a playful side of Blackhawks coach Joel Quenneville that many don't get to see.

Quenneville, 51, will line up one-on-one against his players, usually one of his defensemen, and then battle for control of the puck. It's usually a physical showdown accompanied by smiles and laughter.

"I like playing keep-away with some of the guys — it keeps me in shape," Quenneville said in a recent interview with the Sun-Times.

"I like it more with the 'D.' We're trying them. ... If you got a good stick as a defenseman, it's important."

Of course, keep-away serves a purpose. Quenneville wouldn't be true to himself as a per-

son and a coach if it didn't. It's still practice, after all.

"We always want to be known as the hardest-working team," Quenneville said. "This is a great team to work with. It's a great group of kids."

With Quenneville at the helm, the Hawks are off to one of their best starts in the last 30 years, earning 78 points through 55 games. Their power-play and penalty-kill units and goals-for and goals-against averages rank among the best in the NHL.

Quenneville, though, often uses the word "fortunate" to describe his situation. He'll tell you that he took over the Hawks at an ideal time, with players such as Patrick Kane, Jonathan Toews and Duncan Keith at his disposal, and that he was lucky enough to learn from some of the brightest minds in hockey.

Above: Coach Joel Quenneville directs his team during opening training camp. Richard A. Chapman | Sun-Times

But others, such as Stanley Cup-winning coaches Scotty Bowman and Marc Crawford, will say otherwise. To them, the Hawks' revival is more the result of a perfect marriage between a young and eager-to-learn team and a humble, no-nonsense coach with a sharp approach to the game.

"I just thought he would be a perfect fit for a young team," said Bowman, a Hawks senior adviser who has been part of 11 Stanley Cup-winning teams. "They definitely needed some teaching. They needed some structure, and he was able to give it to them."

PAST THE 'STACHE

In a city filled with colorful coaches and managers, Quenneville maintains a relatively low profile. He doesn't produce the epic rants like the White Sox' Ozzie Guillen or the Cubs' Lou Piniella, nor does he exude the unwavering calmness of the Bears' Lovie Smith.

Quenneville's biggest media splash came when he replaced Hawks legend and Hall of Famer Denis Savard only four games into last season. Now, Quenneville is perhaps best known around these parts for his Mike Ditka-like mustache.

"I don't really worry about accolades or anything like that," said Quenneville, who first was hired by the Hawks as a scout. "I'm not looking for anything other than 'Let's win.'"

Off the ice, Quenneville, a self-described "hacker golfer," enjoys skiing and is passionate about football and horse racing. His Super Bowl pick? The Colts.

His largest earnings at the track? "I've had some major scores," he said, "and I've had some tough days at the office."

On the ice, the native of Windsor, Ontario, is considered one of the sharpest minds in the game — just ask Crawford, the Dallas Stars' coach who won a Stanley Cup with Quenneville in 1996, when they worked for the Colorado Avalanche.

"Joel's best quality is his vision of the game," said Crawford, who had Quenneville as his assistant coach with the St. John's Maple Leafs (AHL), Quebec Nordiques and Avalanche. "They talk about the great athletes having good vision and being able to see the game at a different level. Joel Quenneville has that as a coach.

"Joel almost has a photographic memory on how he sees the game. It is remarkable how accurate he is. He's able to use that vision. He makes his corrections and adapts in the game as well as anybody in the league. Maybe better."

Above: Hawks coach Joel Quenneville watches his team play in the second period. John J. Kim | Sun-Times

JUST BE YOURSELF

Quenneville shrugs off any form of praise or attention, preferring to heap it upon others. When Bowman gives him recognition for his role in improving the Hawks' young defensemen, Quenneville praises the players for their hard work.

"They are doing whatever they can to better themselves," Quenneville said of his defensemen, a group that includes Olympians Keith and Brent Seabrook. "The guys should take all the credit."

You get the sense that is how it always has been for Quenneville, even with his impressive track record. Quenneville replaced Mike Keenan as the St. Louis Blues' head coach midway through the 1996-97 season and led the team to seven consecutive playoff appearances. He won the Jack Adams Award in 2000 as the league's top coach, and he guided the Avalanche to two playoff appearances in three years after leaving the Blues.

"He's very strong on the bench," Bowman said.

"He knows his matchups."

Quenneville credits many individuals for helping lay the foundation for his success, including Crawford, Roger Neilson, Jack Evans, Mike Kitchen, Pat Burns and Darryl Sittler.

"You bring a little bit of something from everyone," Quenneville said. "But the most important thing is that you've got to be yourself and do what you feel is right."

The right choice for Quenneville nearly 20 years ago was accepting the opportunity handed to him by Cliff Fletcher. The former Toronto Maple Leafs general manager offered him the chance to be a player-assistant coach under Crawford with St. John's in 1991. He accepted, and a coaching career was born.

"I was always concerned about getting a real job when I was done playing," said Quenneville, who spent 13 seasons in the NHL as a defenseman, seven with the Hartford Whalers. "The last four years I was playing, I was working as a retail broker with a firm in Hartford, Conn. ... Coaching was the next challenge."

Above: Blackhawk coach Joel Quenneville leading the team through a workout. Rich Hein | Sun-Times

BEYOND THE BENCH

Quenneville's current and former players describe him as

"approachable" and "personable," but also as a person who has his priorities in order.

"Joel's the type of guy who gives the players their space; he respects their environment," said Marc Bergevin, the Hawks' director of player personnel, who played for Quenneville for six seasons with the Blues. "You never felt like Joel was out of control, whether I was playing or when I was an assistant coach last year for the Hawks. Everything is in control with him."

Part of that control is keeping things simple for the young Hawks.

Quenneville makes it clear what their responsibilities are on both ends of the ice and holds them accountable. He also gives everyone a chance to contribute.

The results should speak for themselves.

"He simplifies everything for us," Hawks defenseman Brian Campbell said. "It's kind of nice. It's nothing that's too complicated. He's very persistent in his ways, which once you get caught on to it, it works well for you. He's always seeing what we can do better."

Even if it's competing with him in a game of keep-away.■

A WINNER AT EVERY STOP

Season	Team	W	L	T	OTL	Playoff Result
1996-97	St. Louis	18	15	7	—	Lost in Round 1
1997-98	St. Louis	45	29	8	—	Lost in Round 2
1998-99	St. Louis	37	32	13	—	Lost in Round 2
1999-00	St. Louis	51	19	11	1	Lost in Round 1
2000-01	St. Louis	43	22	12	5	Lost in Round 3
2001-02	St. Louis	43	27	8	4	Lost in Round 2
2002-03	St. Louis	41	24	11	6	Lost in Round 1
2003-04	St. Louis	29	23	7	2	Replaced midseason
2005-06	Colorado	43	30	—	9	Lost in Round 2
2006-07	Colorado	44	31	—	7	Out of playoffs
2007-08	Colorado	44	31	—	7	Lost in Round 2
2008-09	HAWKS	45	22	—	11	Lost in conf. finals
2009-10	HAWKS	37	14	—	4	
TOTAL		**520**	**319**	**77**	**56**	

STANLEY CUP FINALS

GAME 1:   FLYERS 5 | BLACKHAWKS 6

After the dust settled from the first two periods in Game 1 of the Stanley Cup finals, the unlikeliest of players stepped in and played the role of hero.

For the time being, Tomas Kopecky, the spotlight is on you.

Kopecky, a scratch the last five games for the Blackhawks, scored the game-winner at 8:25 in the third period to cap an absolutely wild, up-and-down 6-5 win against the Philadelphia Flyers in the opening game of the best-of-seven series Saturday at the United Center.

"You just can't think, you just got to go out there and react," said Kopecky, who had an assist and was a plus-2 while filling in for an injured Andrew Ladd on the Hawks' checking line of center Dave Bolland and winger Kris Versteeg.

"Right now at this time of the year, it's about who wants it more. Today we played good but we got a long way ahead of us and we got to get ready for Monday [in Game 2].

"I wouldn't say I'm a hero. We got 23 heroes here. Everybody was pulling today, the penalty kill and everybody. Antti [Niemi] was unbelievable again. It's not about one guy right now."

The really unbelievable thing is that neither the Hawks' top line of Patrick Kane, Jonathan

Above: Blackhawk Tomas Kopecky (#82) celebrates after scoring the game-winner.
John J. Kim | Sun-Times

Toews and Dustin Byfuglien nor the Flyers' first line of Mike Richards, Jeff Carter and Simon Gagne factored in any of the 11 goals. All of them had minus ratings.

But unbelievable is exactly what Game 1 was from start to finish.

There were six lead changes in Game 1 which was tied at 5 after two periods. There were a Stanley Cup record-tying five goals scored in the first period, Flyers goalie

Above: Dave Bolland skates toward the Flyers' goal to score short-handed in the first period. John J. Kim | Sun-Times

Michael Leighton was chased in the second during a one-goal game, Bolland scored on another short-handed breakaway and no penalties were called against the always testy Flyers.

"The bottom line is that we won the game and we're moving on to Game 2," said center Patrick Sharp, who had a goal. "I don't think either side is happy with the way things turned out."

Troy Brouwer scored two goals and added an assist, Versteeg and Bolland each had a goal and an assist and Niklas Hjalmarsson and Marian Hossa each had two assists for the Hawks, who trailed 3-2 after the first period.

Danny Briere had a goal and three assists and Scott Hartnell added a goal and two assists to lead the Flyers. Leighton, so strong against the Montreal Canadiens in the Eastern Conference finals, was chased by the Hawks in the second period. The Hawks scored five times on Leighton on 20 shots.

"A lot of action — shootout at the OK Corral," Hawks coach Joel Quenneville said. "Certainly, I don't think anybody envisioned [it being] 5-5 heading into the third period. I still thought we improved as the game went on. That's kind of the niche we want to do."

It was Hawks goalie Niemi who really improved as the game wore on. He shook off some inopportune bounces that led to Flyers goals to shut the door in the third period. He finished with 27 saves.

Brian Boucher, the Flyers' playoff starter who was hurt in the Boston Bruins series, relieved Leighton and allowed one goal on 12 shots. That one goal was Kopecky's.

"You get all that energy just kind of watching the guys," Kopecky said. "You just got to keep your head up and keep working hard and keep yourself in it."

He did that in Game 1.∎

This wasn't a Stanley Cup finals game. Couldn't be. Those games tend to be serious, strategic, defensive affairs.

This? This was the Home Run Derby at baseball's All-Star Game. This was the Pebble Beach Pro-Am.

This was insane.

If you like to buy your goals in bulk, the United Center was the place to be Saturday night. If you like low-scoring games, well, the Phillies' Roy Halladay did throw a 1-0 perfect game earlier in the evening.

No, this most certainly wasn't that. The Blackhawks and the Flyers opened their series with a bang. And a bang. And a bang.

By the time the shooting was over, it was 6-5 Hawks, with the home team grabbing a 1-0 lead in this Stanley Cup finals. Was it sloppy? Gloriously so.

"Shootout at the OK Corral," Hawks coach Joel Quenneville said.

Resistance was futile. Goalie self-esteem was at an all-time low.

But Hawks goaltender Antti Niemi did grab a blazing slap shot from Danny Briere with about two minutes left in the game. And when the Flyers pulled their goalie for a man advantage in the final minute, the Hawks did a masterful job of stuffing, slowing and otherwise impeding the progress of the puck.

The buzzer went off, the ship horn sounded three times and The Fratellis' "Chelsea Dagger"— the Hawks' goal and victory song — turned the crowd of 22,312 people into dancing fools. The Fratellis made some serious royalty money Saturday night.

This series isn't going to be easy. But it could be very, very fun.

Before the second period was over, Philly goalie Michael Leighton was gone, having let in five of 20 shots. Brian Boucher was called to duty, and he

Above: Chicago Blackhawks center Dave Bolland (36) salutes cheering fans, including actor Vince Vaughn, third from left in the front row, after Bolland scored. Nam Y. Huh | AP Photo

actually accepted the challenge. A lesser goalie might have seen the carnage and left the building.

Neither team got up by more than a goal in this game. What were the odds of the Hawks scoring six goals and neither Patrick Kane nor Jonathan Toews having a point? That's how crazy it was.

Crazy is good, to a point.

"It's a real emotional game," said forward Troy Brouwer, who scored twice for the Hawks. "[A] lot of back and forth, a lot of up and down. You just try to stay composed."

Marian Hossa, his linemate, was spectacular. The knock on him has been that he hasn't scored enough goals in the playoffs. But he made a pass from behind the net that could make a hockey purist cry tears of joy, sliding the puck to Brouwer, who put it past Leighton. That made it 5-4.

Hossa assisted on both of Brouwer's goals.

"He just kept getting open," said Hossa, who was plus-1 in the humility department.

Tomas Kopecky was outstanding, as well, with a sweet pass on a Kris Versteeg goal and the game-winning goal 8:25 into the third period.

That might have been the most amazing thing about this game. After a blizzard of 11 goals, neither team scored in the last 11:35. Niemi lost his helmet a couple times in the third period, but not his head.

Afterward, the Hawks were talking about momentum. The Flyers were not. The losing team doesn't want to acknowledge the existence of momentum.

"The first game is always big because you want to get the momentum going," Hossa said. "... It's all about momentum in the finals."

This was a huge game for the Hawks. They haven't always played well at home in the postseason, and they haven't always started well. They weren't great Saturday night. In fact, there were spans when they weren't very good at all. But they were good enough. And entertaining.

Did we mention entertaining?

The Flyers had 17 shots on goal in the first period. Let me repeat that: 17 shots. Niemi looked like the guy in the caged cart retrieving golf balls at the driving range.

The most egregious goal was the third one of the period for the Flyers. There were four Hawks in front of Niemi when Briere skated in and lifted a rebound into the net. Let me repeat that: There were four Blackhawks and no Flyers in front of Niemi when Briere got to the puck.

That goal occurred with 27 seconds left in the period, meaning the Hawks' locker room must have so very pleasant when Quenneville shut the door.

It was Briere who had intercepted a bad Brian Campbell pass to set up the Flyers' first goal.

The Hawks didn't have a monopoly on mistakes. Dave Bolland took a bouncing puck away from Philadelphia's Braydon Coburn and scored on a breakaway to give the Hawks a 2-1 lead.

The Hawks played better in the third period, and that included Kane, who was almost invisible for the first two periods.

"I thought we had more speed in our game," Quenneville said of the third.

There was some good news for the Hawks' top line. Toews was 12-for-12 on face-offs in the first period. But Kane, Toews and Dustin Byfuglien will need to have an impact in Game 2 on Monday night.

The Flyers are going to try to tighten up their game. They don't want to get caught up in a track meet. Can you have a track meet on ice?

"We were just too loose in front of our net," Flyers coach Peter Laviolette said.

If the Hawks can win the first two games at the United Center, they are going to be extremely difficult to beat. They are not the Bruins, after all. And they're not the Canadiens.

They're the Hawks, and they're now three victories from a Stanley Cup.■

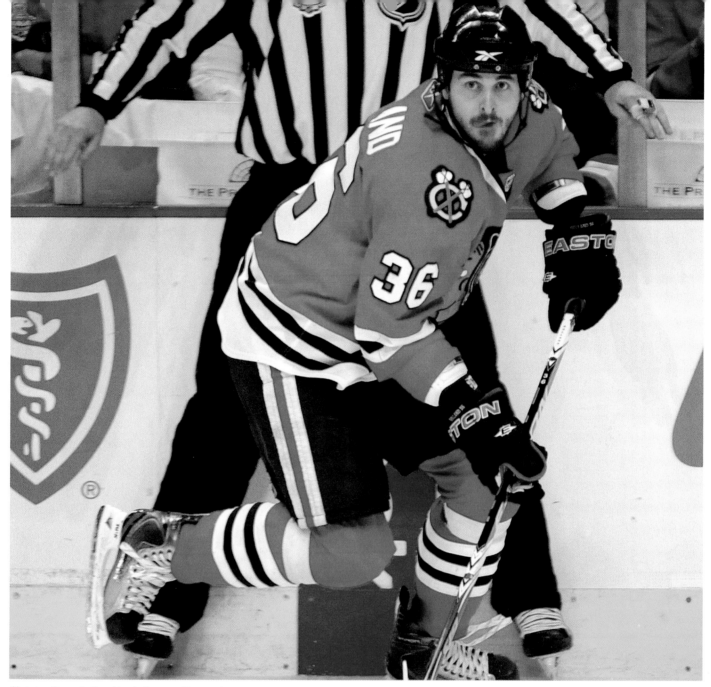

Above: Dave Bolland looks to pass the puck. John J. Kim | Sun-Times

★ THREE STARS ★

★ TOMAS KOPECKY

The Blackhawks winger went from a scratch to the limelight in a matter of days by scoring the game-winner in the third period. Kopecky, who sat out the last five games, had an assist and a plus-2 rating while taking the place of injured Andrew Ladd on the Hawks' checking line of Dave Bolland and Kris Versteeg.

★ TROY BROUWER

The winger scored twice for the Hawks on two nice passes by Marian Hossa. Brouwer also assisted on Patrick Sharp's goal on a breakout in the second period. The second line of Hossa, Brouwer and Sharp combined for three goals and six points in Game 1, making up for minus-3 nights by the Hawks' top line of Jonathan Toews, Patrick Kane and Dustin Byfuglien.

★ DANNY BRIERE

The Flyers center put a ton of pressure on Hawks goalie Antti Niemi with a game-high six shots on goal. Briere finished with a goal and three assists and was noticeable throughout the game. He endured a big check from Byfuglien with 1:11 left in the second period to set up Arron Asham's goal that tied the game at 5.

Two very different games. Two frantic finishes. Two close wins by the Blackhawks.

Only two more to go.

The Hawks opened a two-goal lead and then held off a third-period flurry by the Flyers for a 2-1 victory in Game 2 of the Stanley Cup finals — winning both games at the United Center to maintain home-ice advantage with two games ahead in Philadelphia.

"They're not going to go away," Hawks center Patrick Sharp said of the Flyers. "They have so much talent. We got to keep getting better. I thought we showed a lot of composure, a lot of poise. We dug in there and battled pretty hard.

"There is a reason why these two teams are in the finals, and I think every game is going to be pretty tight going forward. We managed to hang on to a one-goal victory in both games. Hopefully, we can keep doing it."

Marian Hossa and Ben Eager scored 28 seconds apart late in the second period to open a 2-0 lead, and Antti Niemi stood his ground all game making 32 saves, including 14 during a furious third period.

For Hossa, scoring for the first time since May 5 against the Vancouver Canucks during the Western Conference semifinals was a huge relief.

Above: Tomas Kopecky, left, exchanges words with Daniel Carcillo in the first period after Carcillo went for a big hit on Kopecky, but missed.   John J. Kim | Sun-Times

"It's been a long time," said Hossa, who continued to make an impact in other aspects of the game. "I just tried to work hard. I was looking for some ugly goal like that to get the offense going."

Hossa jumped on one of the few rebounds yielded by Michael Leighton, who made 24 saves after being chased in Game 1 by allowing five goals on 20 shots.

"[Hossa] can stop answering all those questions now," said Sharp, who missed an empty-netter in the final minute. "He does so much

Above: Chicago Blackhawks right wing Marian Hossa scores to give the Hawks the first lead of the game. Scott Stewart | Sun-Times

out there in all areas that he's a huge part of our team. He did what he does best tonight by putting the puck in the net."

Eager then beat Leighton with a wrist shot from the left circle for a 2-0 lead as the Hawks continued to get production from nearly all their players.

The Flyers made it 2-1 on Simon Gagne's power-play goal at 5:20 of the third period. But that was all the Flyers could muster against Niemi and a strong effort from the Hawks' defense.

All the pressure suited the Hawks just fine - even if they were outshot 15-4 in the third period.

"It's a 2-1 lead; it's a close game," defenseman Duncan Keith said. "They are pressing for a goal. So there's pressure on them to score, and there's pressure on us to defend. I would rather be in our position trying to defend.

"They had some chances there and Antti made some nice plays, took up a lot of the

net. We did a good job of clearing some pucks out to not let them get any rebounds."

It all added up to the Hawks' seventh consecutive victory this postseason.

"Their goaltender played extremely well in the third period," Flyers coach Peter Laviolette said. "We had more than enough looks to tie up that game."

The defensive lapses and breakdowns that led to a frantic, high-scoring affair in Game 1 were not as plentiful in Game 2. The biggest goal for both teams was tightening up in their own zones, and they did that for the most part.

The Hawks set the tone early with 20 hits in the first period and even got their first power plays of the series after going without in the first game.

"Games are going to get tougher," veteran center John Madden said. "We know how they play in their building.

"Game 3 is a huge game."∎

This feels over. This feels done, finished, complete, triple filtered and whatever word means "the Flyers will receive a lovely parting gift."

The Blackhawks will tell you otherwise because that's what they're supposed to do. Their 2-1 victory Monday night means they have a commanding 2-0 lead in the Stanley Cup finals.

But you won't hear that from them.

They're going to tell you that there's no quit in the lads from Philadelphia, and they might even be right.

But the United Center was supposed to be the hard part for the Hawks, right? They had a recent postseason history of tensing up in familiar territory. They tended to move at home with the ease of people who had slept on beds of nails.

Well, guess what? The Hawks won the first two games of this series, which now moves to Philadelphia for Games 3 and 4. They have won seven straight road playoff games.

And they won the first two home games in disparate ways.

If you can come up with a reason the Flyers have a chance besides their propensity for improbable comebacks, let's hear it.

The Hawks are not the Bruins, who blew a 3-0 series lead against the Flyers. And they're not Montreal, which lost in the Eastern Conference finals to the Flyers.

They're the Hawks, and now Philadelphia knows exactly what that means. They can play poorly and still win 6-5, as they did in Game 1. And they can tighten up their game, absorb punishment, hand out their own abuse and win that way too.

That was Game 2.

So what will the Flyers try in Game 3 Wednesday night? Rollerblades and the power of persuasion?

No, the Flyers have too much to solve and not enough time or talent to do it.

But you won't hear that from them.

"I'm not sure we should be frustrated," Philly coach Peter Laviolette said. "I don't think we got outplayed."

This game started the way you would expect after a high-scoring Game 1. It started scoreless and stayed that way for a long, long time.

Somewhere between the conspicuous consumption of Game 1 and the hunger strike of most of the first two periods of Game 2, there had to be a happy medium.

Those of us who actually like scoring and aren't ashamed of saying so wanted a bone thrown our way.

It arrived suddenly. Marian Hossa knocked in a rebound with about three minutes left in the second period to make it 1-0. And before the public-address announcer could run down the scoring and assists, Ben Eager had beaten Philly goalie Michael Leighton with a blistering wrist shot to make it 2-0.

Hossa, the guy who couldn't buy a goal for the longest time in these playoffs.

"It's been a long time," he said, smiling.

Eager, the guy who can make the bell ring at the circus but isn't known for his scoring prowess.

"A huge goal," coach Joel Quenneville said.

The scary part Monday night was the way the Hawks tightened up after the Flyers' Simon Gagne scored to cut the lead to 2-1 with about 15 minutes left in the game. The Hawks spent too much time on the back of their skates.

"We certainly didn't want to spend that much time in our own end," Quenneville said.

If not for the stellar work of Antti Niemi in the net for the Hawks, this might have been a different story. But he was excellent all night, especially in the last 10 minutes. Hard to believe he hadn't played in a postseason game until this season.

"Maybe it's better he has no experience," Eager said. "He just shows up to play every night."

Right from the beginning, you could tell that both teams wanted to atone for the scoring fest that was Game 1, as if a combined 11 goals was against everything that was good and right and true about hockey.

They were embarrassed, and they seemed to feel the need to apologize not just to the fans but to all the former players out there who had rolled their eyes Saturday night and wondered out loud what was wrong with today's youth.

That much scoring points to fanciness, and from there, it's a short trip to dainty and delicate.

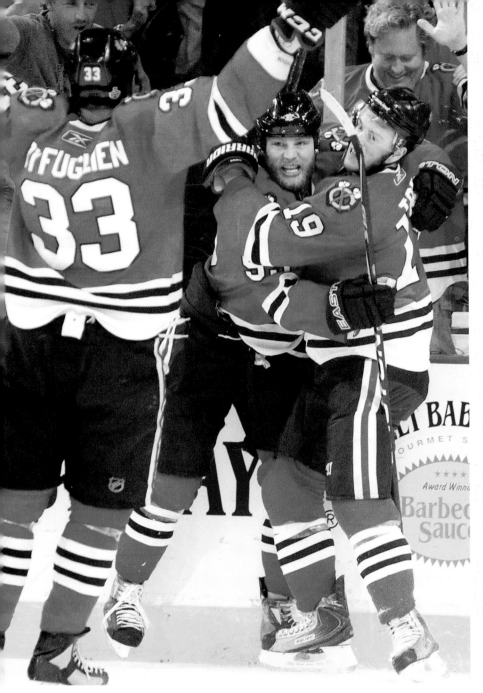

Above: Ben Eager, middle, is congratulated after scoring. John J. Kim | Sun-Times

So they came out hitting Monday night. If you like your hockey raw, you were in heaven. The Flyers managed to get just three shots on net in a 0-0 first period.

This was an ode to brutality. Philadelphia's Jeff Carter and Daniel Carcillo approached the Hawks' Tomas Kopecky from opposite sides, with the intent of reducing him to processed meat. But they ran into each other instead, and the collision caused Carter to be separated from his helmet.

The Flyers' Chris Pronger gave Jonathan Toews a vicious shove with his stick after a whistle. It was like that Monday night, all menace and evil intent.

Yes, the Hawks did manage to get a power play, after getting none in Game 1. The first one came almost 15 minutes into the game, a cross-checking call on Blair Betts, and the UC crowd roared both in appreciation and in derision of the officiating in the first game.

Unlike in Game 1, Toews and Patrick Kane were factors Monday night. Toews, in particular, was all over the ice. Surely, it would lead to something. But it didn't.

And that's Reason No. 8 or 9 the Flyers are in trouble: neither Toews nor Kane has a point yet.

No matter.

Two down, two to go.∎

★ THREE STARS ★

★ ANTTI NIEMI

After allowing five goals in Game 1, he came up big when the Hawks needed it most yet again — stopping 32 of 33 shots to salvage a victory out of an improved, but still uneven, performance by the Hawks. Got stronger as the game went on, stopping 14 of 15 shots in the third period.

★ MARIAN HOSSA

Rewarded for his persistence with a goal on a rebound that gave the Hawks a 1-0 lead with 2:51 left in the second period. It was Hossa's third goal of the postseason and first in eight games. But he also has 14 points in 18 postseason games.

★ BEN EAGER

Fourth-line forward parlayed the momentum from Hossa's goal into one of his own, firing a wicked shot past Michael Leighton to give the Hawks a 2-0 lead just 28 seconds after Hossa's goal. It was Eager's first goal of the playoffs, the second of his career and typical of the contributions the Hawks have received from their supporting cast throughout the postseason. Scored while playing with Jonathan Toews and Dustin Byfuglien.

STANLEY CUP FINALS

GAME 3:   BLACKHAWKS 3 | FLYERS 4 (OT)

The never-say-quit Philadelphia Flyers never quit in Game 3 of the Stanley Cup finals. Nothing, it seemed, could derail the inevitable. Not goal reviews. Not unfortunate bounces. Nothing.

The result is a more interesting finals as the Flyers prevailed 4-3 in overtime Wednesday at the Wachovia Center. Claude Giroux redirected in the game-winner at 5:59 in overtime.

"There were spurts where we did what we wanted to, but at the same time, there were spurts when we didn't," defenseman Brent Sopel said.

"At the end of the day, it's over. It's done with. There's nothing you can do but move on to Game 4."

Giroux added two assists, and Scott Hartnell had a goal and an assist to the lead the Flyers, who improved to a league-best 8-1 at home in the playoffs. Danny Briere also had a goal.

The game-winner came less than a minute after Simon Gagne's bad-angle shot deflected off Dave Bolland's stick and off the far post and literally rolled over the goal line before Niemi was able to cover it. The horn sounded and a review ensued, but it was ruled no good.

It was the second goal review for the Flyers. Hartnell's power-play goal was reviewed minutes after it appeared to just barely cross the goal line. Unlike Gagne's, it did cross the line.

"There was no doubt in my mind that we were going to find a way," Briere said. "They

Above: Referee Bill McCreary waits for the answer on the Flyers overtime goal that was taken away after a video review.   Scott Stewart | Sun-Times

even let us celebrate twice. So that was nice."

Game 3 was a mix of the first two games. It was wide-open at times with each team getting quality scoring chances but failing to convert, and tight and physical during other stretches.

According to the scoresheet, the Flyers did many of things that usually equate to victories:

■They took advantage on special teams and converted on the power play twice. "Stay out of the box and don't give them an opportunity," Sopel said.

Above: Blackhawks goaltender Antti Niemi watches as the puck sails into the net while the Flyers Claude Giroux watches his game-winner in overtime. Scott Stewart | Sun-Times

■ They established a physical edge against the Hawks 40-31, including some jarring hits by Flyers defenseman Chris Pronger.

■They had the advantage in the face-off circle, winning 55 percent of the draws overall and 61 percent through three periods. The Flyers had issues within the circles in the first two games.

■They outshot the Hawks 15-4 in the third period — the same totals from Game 2. "The more we hold on to the pucks in their zone, it's going to be tougher to score," Hawks winger Tomas Kopecky said of negating the Flyers' third-period success. "We just have to protect the puck a little more and keep cycling."

■They also killed off three Hawks power plays, allowing only five shots to reach goalie Michael Leighton (24 saves). "I think we got to

have a little bit more movement and shoot the puck," defenseman Duncan Keith said. "We're trying to be a little too cute at times."

Patrick Kane found the scoresheet for the first time in the series with a goal and an assist for the Hawks, who overcame two one-goal deficits.

Kane's breakaway goal 2:50 into the third gave the Hawks a 3-2 lead, but the Flyers answered 20 seconds later when Ville Leino put a rebound past Antti Niemi (28 saves).

Keith and Sopel also scored. Keith's goal deflected off Jeff Carter's stick and went in, and Sopel's, coming after John Madden won a draw, also appeared to be redirected.

"That was the kind of game you'd expect in the Stanley Cup finals from a team down 2-0," Hawks winger Adam Burish said. "They played a good game. Give them credit."■

Philadelphia Flyers winger Scott Hartnell and Blackhawks winger Tomas Kopecky have words as the linesman break up their scrap.
Scott Stewart | Sun-Times

The crowd was fired up. If it squinted hard enough, it could see the fortunes of its beloved team changing Wednesday night.

It so wanted to believe in magic. It wanted to believe that something beyond talent and effort had pushed the Flyers through their improbable playoff run, and would do so again. So what if the Blackhawks had won the first two games of this Stanley Cup finals? There's no magic unless there's a rabbit and a hat, right?

For their part, the Hawks not only wanted to beat the Flyers in Game 3, they wanted to debunk them.

Magic gets a grudging nod this time.

Claude Giroux redirected Matt Carle's shot past the Hawks' Antti Niemi 5 minutes, 59 seconds into overtime to give Philadelphia a 4-3 victory and a lungful of new life.

So, yes, there will be talk of the Flyers' aura today, that indefinable something that helped them get into the playoffs on a shootout goal in the last game of the regular season and helped them come back from a 3-0 playoff series deficit against the Bruins.

"We find a way to get it done," Giroux said.

But it's also true that the Hawks got caught in a shift change in overtime, leading to Giroux's game-winner.

There's magic, and then there's reality. Only twice in 33 Stanley Cup finals has a team down 2-0 come back to win the series.

The Hawks know this. They also know that they battled Wednesday night and have every reason to believe they should have won Game 3.

They still control this series. The Flyers think otherwise.

"They probably felt they could have won tonight," Philly coach Peter Laviolette said. "We felt we could have won the first two games."

"If you had said we'd be up 2-1 after three games, we probably would have taken it," the Hawks' Adam Burish said.

Luck? Magic? If the Hawks had won this game, we'd be talking about all the fortuitous things that had happened to them Wednesday night.

In overtime, Simone Gagne's shot clanged off a goalpost, and the puck skidded along the goal line. Magic would have turned it toward the net. Reality had Niemi getting his glove on it before it could do the Hawks any harm.

No lack of rough stuff

If you want to get down to it, this game was more about nastiness than it was about sleight of hand. This was a mean, harsh affair. It's what happens when two teams play each other several times in a row. It's what happens when men carry sticks.

Flyers defenseman Chris Pronger and his elbows, forearms and hockey stick were everywhere. It had to be this way because nothing had worked for Philadelphia in Games 1 and 2.

The Flyers were down 2-0 in the series, not much had been going right, so out came the elbows. Pronger dropped Jonathan Toews with one. Gloves to the face after the whistle were a favorite, too.

Even the diminutive Patrick Kane took a halfhearted swing at Giroux after a whistle early in the game. And it was Kane who was in the middle of a scrum at the end of the first period. He ended up without his helmet, and teammate Dustin Byfuglien ended up in the penalty box for protecting him.

At the end of Game 2, Pronger had picked up the puck before Ben Eager could get to it to keep for his trophy case. That led to words between the two and 10-minute misconduct penalties.

So here we were for Game 3, and it was as rough as expected.

The Flyers had not been subtle about their intentions heading into Game 3. Laviolette had tried to get inside Niemi's head.

Above: The Blackhawks' Patrick Kane, left, celebrates with Jonathan Toews after scoring in the third period. John J. Kim | Sun-Times

Opposite Page: Blackhawks winger Dustin Byfuglien had to be held back by the linesman after being called for a penalty against Flyers instigator Chris Pronger. Scott Stewart | Sun-Times

★ THREE STARS ★

★ CLAUDE GIROUX
The young right winger scored the game-winner when he deflected a shot past Antti Niemi at 5:59 of the first overtime. Giroux also added an assist when he looked to make a cross-slot pass in the second period that was redirected toward Niemi. The Blackhawks goalie made the save but allowed Ville Leino to score on the rebound.

★ SCOTT HARTNELL
The bruising left wing scored a controversial goal to give his team a brief 2-1 lead midway through the second period when officials ruled that his shot indeed had crossed the goal line. Hartnell also added an assist when he helped set up a Danny Briere goal that gave the Flyers a 1-0 lead 14:58 into the first period.

★ PATRICK KANE
Neutralized during the first two games in the United Center, Kane scored his first goal of the Stanley Cup finals on a breakaway at 2:50 of the third period. Earlier, he found himself with rare time and space and helped set up a Duncan Keith goal that tied the score at 2:49 of the second period.

"He's representing a city that hasn't had a Cup in 50 years," he had said. "We have to give him a crack of doubt. We can do that [in Game 3]."

Niemi was fine. The Flyers didn't get to him. I don't know what would get to him. A hockey stick with Taser-like properties?

It took a replay to give the Flyers a 2-1 lead in the second period. Scott Hartnell's shot had slid past Niemi, and as the puck got to the goal line, Niklas Hjalmarsson reached in with his stick and dug it out. But the replay clearly showed the puck crossing the line, and every time the play was shown from a different angle on the arena scoreboard, the crowd roared. So when the announcement finally was made that it was indeed a goal, the place rocked.

Hawks have some magic, too.

And you couldn't blame the fans for believing something had changed. It looked pivotal, possibly momentous. They had seen some crazy things on a wild playoff ride, so why not a slippery goal that knocked the wind out of the Hawks?

Because it didn't happen that way. The Hawks came back in the second to make it 2-2 on a goal by Brent Sopel.

Brent Sopel!

If you want to talk about magic, there it is. The defenseman scored one goal in 73 regular-season games. He matched that with a shot from above the circle off a faceoff won by John Madden.

Immediately after, it was so quiet at the Wachovia Center, you could have heard a puck drop.

And when Kane scored off a breakaway early in the third, a depression settled over the crowd. Toews got the assist, his first point in three Cup games.

Sopel, a man in the shadows, had scored. So had Kane, a man who lives for the spotlight.

So there were a number of reasons to imagine that the Flyers would simply go away. But this is hockey and these are hockey players. A puck bounced around and bounced around some more until it landed on the stick of Ville Leino, who beat Niemi for a goal that tied it 3-3.

That set up the dramatic overtime. Is there any other kind of overtime? Yes, the Flyers would say. A magical one. ∎

NOT SINCE 1961

The similarity is not lost upon Bobby Hull.

In 1961, the soon-to-be Golden Jet was 22 and teammate Stan Mikita was 20, two young stars charged with lifting the Blackhawks out of a dark age. And it happened sooner than anybody thought.

After upsetting the five-time defending champion Montreal Canadiens 4-2 in the Stanley Cup semifinals, the Blackhawks cruised past the Detroit Red Wings to win their first Stanley Cup since 1938. Not bad for a team that had reached the playoffs only once in 12 seasons from 1947-58.

"The fact that Jonathan Toews is the leader of this team at 22 and Patrick Kane being one of the goal scorers they depend on, it was very much the same kind of deal in '61 when we won the Cup," Hull said. "Mikita was young and a future Hall of Famer at that age. I was 22 and I could skate all night. They had to rope me down to stop me."

The 1961 Hawks were a similar mixture of youth and experience. Hull led the team with 31 goals. Mikita scored 19. Wingers Murray Balfour (21 goals) and Ab McDonald (17) and defenseman Reggie Fleming were 24. Center Bill Hay, who led the team with 59 points, was 25. Wingers Ron Murphy (21 goals), Eric Nesterenko (19) and Kenny Wharram (16) were 27. And two future Hall of Famers, defenseman Pierre Pilote and goaltender Glenn Hall, were 29.

And they had just won their first Stanley Cup. And their last. The Hawks reached the finals the following year but lost to the Toronto Maple Leafs 4-2. They returned to the finals in 1965 and lost to the Canadiens 4-3. They made it in 1971 and lost an excruciating finals series to the Canadiens, 4-3. After Hull left for the World Hockey Association, Mikita made it one more time in 1973, but the Hawks lost to the Canadiens again, this time 4-2.

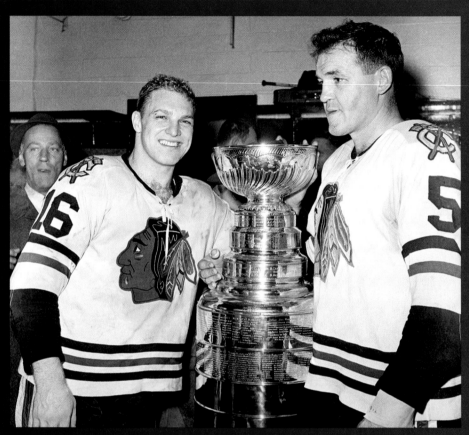

Above: This April 16, 1961, file photo shows Chicago Blackhawks' Bobby Hull, left, and Jack Evans flanking the Stanley Cup in their dressing room in Detroit after defeating the Detroit Red Wings to win the Cup. As Chicago inched toward its first Stanley Cup championship in 49 years, Hull had some advice. "Take advantage of it now. You're so very close." AP Photo

"I figured that the 1961 Cup was just going to be one of many that we were going to win during our span in the National Hockey League," Hull said. "I was too young to really appreciate how important it was to win that Cup.

"That's what I'm trying to get across to the kids today — you are so close that if you don't take advantage of this, you may regret it for years to come."

The Blackhawks were an upstart winner in 1961. They were 29-24-17 in the regular season, finishing third in the six-team NHL with 75 points, 17 behind the Canadiens. But they stunned the Canadiens in the semifinals, winning the series 4-2 against a team that had swept them 4-0 and outscored them 14-6 the previous year.

Murray Balfour's goal in the third overtime in

Above: This April 16, 1961, file photo shows a jubilant Bobby Hull of the Chicago Blackhawks, left, shouting to a fan in the final moments of the Blackhawks Stanley Cup victory against the Detroit Red Wings, in Detroit. At right is teammate Eric Nesterenko. AP Photo

Game 3 at the Stadium gave the Hawks a 2-1 series lead.

"That was the turning point," Mikita said. "That's when we thought we could beat the Canadiens. I was playing the point and I wanted to take a shot on goal. Somebody came right at me, so I slid the puck to Murray Balfour and got away from his check and slammed it home."

The Canadiens won 5-2 to tie the series 2-2. But Hall almost singlehandedly took over, shutting out the Canadiens in back-to-back 3-0 victories to clinch it.

"That was unheard of in hockey, especially in those days," Mikita said.

"After that we didn't care who was waiting for us," Hull said. "We knew we had won the Stanley Cup by beating the mighty Montreal Canadiens in the semifinals."

Momentum did the rest. The Hawks beat the Red Wings 4-2 in the finals, winning the final two ames 6-3 and 5-1, with McDonald's goal the game-winner in Game 6 in Detroit.

Penalty killers Fleming, Nesterenko and Earl Balfour and veteran defenders Jack Adams and Arbour — who later won four Stanley Cups as the coach of the New York Islanders from 1979-83 — were the unsung heroes.

Hull's only regret is that he didn't fully appreciate it until later in his career.

"But I want to tell you — I'm ready this time," he said. "The only ones who will be enjoying this more than me will be the guys down there sweating it out, winning the games."∎

STANLEY CUP FINALS

GAME 4:   BLACKHAWKS 3 | FLYERS 5

In overtime of Game 3 of the Stanley Cup finals, center Dave Bolland and wingers Kris Versteeg and Tomas Kopecky — the Blackhawks' checking line — took the draw against the Philadelphia Flyers' Claude Giroux, Danny Briere and Arron Asham.

Duncan Keith and Brent Seabrook also were on the ice for the Hawks as were the Flyers' Chris Pronger and Matt Carle.

But a decision was reached on the Hawks' bench. A line change was to be made. After Giroux won the draw against Bolland, Kopecky and Versteeg skated to the bench and two parts of the Hawks' top line, Patrick Kane and Dustin Byfuglien, came on.

Above: Chicago Blackhawks goalie Antti Niemi cools off in the second period.
Matt Slocum | AP Photo

The switch was too late. The Flyers were already on a rush — and they basically had a 5-on-3 advantage. The result was Giroux's game-winner at 5:59 in overtime. There was nothing Keith, Seabrook or Bolland could really do.

The play is another example of the chess games that go on as Hawks coach Joel Quenneville and Flyers coach Peter Laviolette look for advantageous matchups. It can be the difference between wins and losses, and it gets magnified now, especially when the change leads to a loss.

"Maybe we could've just had one guy change

on the play instead of two, which gave them a little extra man on the rush," Quenneville said Thursday at the Wachovia Center.

"I don't want to get too technical. We don't want to point fingers.

When you're trying to match lines, sometimes you're going to be vulnerable to a tough change. Sometimes there's too many men.

Sometimes a guy gets a late change coming off the bench as well. So that's all part of it. In a situation like that, I'll take the hit for it."

It's established that Bolland's line and the Seabrook-Keith pairing will see plenty of Mike Richards, Jeff Carter and Simon Gagne, three of the Flyers' best offensive players, and that

Above: The Blackhawks watch the game in the final seconds of the third period. John J. Kim | Sun-Times

Pronger and Carle will get a full dose of Jonathan Toews, Kane and Byfuglien.

But Quenneville alluded to another Flyers line Thursday that the Hawks might have to take a more active role against with certain matchups. According to the numbers, that line would be Briere's, which typically consists of Scott Hartnell and Ville Leino, although Laviolette has rotated Giroux and Briere on other lines.

"One line gets a little hotter. Maybe you get away from that, and on the other side, that line might get hot again," Quenneville said. "Sometimes it's a give-and-take. ... Bolland's line is trying to work the one situation. They're doing a decent job. The other times, sometimes you're looking for the 'D' matchups. We'll look at what we can do to slow down one of the other lines and hopefully get more consistency in that area."

Quenneville was adept at pushing the right buttons in the conference finals against the San Jose Sharks, a deep team. But the Flyers have been a bit tougher to figure.

Just as the Hawks' speed and depth have factored in the minus ratings Carter, Richards and Gagne have in the series, the same things can be said about the Flyers.

Briere, Hartnell and Leino all said Thursday that they face Toews, Kane and Byfuglien the most. Together, the Flyers trio has combined for six goals and 14 points, which also includes some power-play success, in the series.

"They're playing really loose," Toews said of Briere's line.

"Things are clicking for them. We just need to be a little more aware because they're supporting each other. They're working hard.

"So we have to try to take that confidence away from that line. We know they've been a big part of that team's success in their offense in the last three games. Maybe we'll have to focus on them a little bit more. More than we have."▪

★ THREE STARS ★

★ VILLE LEINO
After absorbing a crunching hit from Brian Campbell that forced him from the ice, the rookie gave his team a commanding 4-1 lead early in the third period when his high wrister bounced off Kris Versteeg and past Hawks goalie Antti Niemi.

★ CHRIS PRONGER
The veteran didn't score a goal or record an assist, but still finished with a team-high plus-4 rating for the Flyers. The defenseman has been a big reason why Jonathan Toews has yet to score a goal in the first four games. Toews, thanks largely to Pronger, finished minus-2 on Friday.

★ MIKE RICHARDS
The Flyers captain scored his first goal of the series when he stripped Niklas Hjalmarsson as he was trying to clear the puck up the boards and backhanded it past Niemi five seconds into the Flyers' second power play of the game to give the hosts a 1-0 lead.

Uh-oh. I think I heard the entire city of Chicago make that sound.

Uh-oh, as in, "You mean, the Blackhawks aren't going to sweep these losers from Philly?"

Uh-oh, as in, "Get beat tonight at the Wachovia Center and it's a .500 Stanley Cup series?"

Uh-oh, as in "Remember the 2003 playoff Cubs?"

No, we'll stop interpretations of Uh-oh right there. Unfair. There is no Mark Prior on the Hawks. No Dusty Baker on the bench. No Alex Gonzalez at shortstop. No Steve Bar — Stop.

(Evil Rick: Think a ghostlike Steve Bartman might be flashing in the mind of John McDonough, current Blackhawks president, former Cubs president?)

Like crabgrass, hockey doubt has appeared in our town.

That 4-3 overtime loss did it.

The Hawks' sweep of the tough San Jose Sharks in the Western Conference finals now seems like a dream.

Abruptly, Hawks fans have discovered that the Flyers are a terrific power-play team, third best in the NHL in the regular season.

The Flyers also are a great penalty-killing team, with 27 short-handed stops out of 28 in their last two series.

Chicagoans have realized the big, strong, skillful lug Chris Pronger might be a bigger (OK, taller), stronger, more skillful lug than the Hawks' Dustin Byfuglien.

Remember when Big Buff would simply park himself in front of the crease like a bank safe and score the game-winning goal over and over? Hmm, just last series, wasn't it?

Pronger, the Flyers' 35-year-old vet, has moved Buff around and flustered him and done stuff that only a very savvy man could do.

Amazing that a guy like Pronger seems to be everywhere on the ice, creating mayhem, averaging more than 30 minutes a game, snatching the postgame puck, and doing it against Chicago's young-kid team.

How?

Shouldn't an old man who has played for five teams in 16 NHL seasons, who started his pro career with the Peterborough Petes in 1991, be exhausted?

Doubt.

It's not overwhelming. But for the first time in a long time, it's here.

Asked Thursday if he thought he was frustrating Byfuglien, Pronger said, "I don't know. I think you just got to continue denying the easy access to the front of the net and make him work hard for every inch out there. You can ask him."

Hissy, hissy.

The fact is there were Chicago fans who thought Flyers power forward Scott Hartnell — he of the medieval hair and beard — was just some sort of curly-locked caveman. He's not. Even though they have held "Hartnell Wig Night" in Philadelphia, distributing things that look like giant lint balls for fans' heads, Hartnell is, in fact, a swift-skating tornado who, like Pronger, always seems to be where the action is.

This uncertainty all comes around to a simple hockey fact: The Hawks have not won a Stanley Cup in almost a half century, and nobody in Chicago can tell us what it is like to do so.

Love Bobby Hull, Stan Mikita and pals, but there were only six teams in the league when the Hawks won the Cup in 1961. Now there are five times that.

It's hard to compare any team to one like the Flyers that has changed strategy, switched coaches, used several goalies, lost and gained injured players, come together with, as winger Danny Briere says prettily, "chemistry" that "clicks."

The Flyers were a seventh seed that came back from a shocking three-game deficit in the conference semifinals to advance.

If they win this Cup, they will be the sports team story of the year. No doubt about it.

Uh-oh.∎

STANLEY CUP FINALS

GAME 5:   FLYERS 4 | BLACKHAWKS 7

It was the type of effort you'd expect to see from a Stanley Cup champion. And with it, the Blackhawks are just one victory away from being just that.

The energy level was elevated. The power play was productive. The penalty kill was effective. The passes were crisp. The lines were clicking. The breakouts were fast.

Many things were simply better for the Blackhawks in Game 5 of the Stanley Cup finals as they defeated the Philadelphia Flyers 7-4 on Sunday night before a hungry 22,305 at the United Center.

Dustin Byfuglien finally arrived in the finals, scoring twice and recording two assists and nine hits to lead the Hawks, who made an emphatic statement with a dominating opening period after suffering back-to-back losses in Philadelphia.

Six players scored and 11 players notched at least a point for the Hawks, who now lead the best-of-seven finals with three wins — all of them at the United Center. Game 6 is Wednesday in Philadelphia.

"We knew that our time was due," Bolland said. "We knew that this was going to come out sooner than later. We didn't see it in the first or second games or the third or fourth.

Above: Joey Kuhl, age 9 from Elmhurst, shows his support to the Blackhawks before game No.5 of the Stanley Cup Final. Scott Stewart | Sun-Times

Tonight we sort of brought it together and played well."

It seemed as if everyone played well at times in Game 5. When some Hawks struggled and the Flyers capitalized, others stepped up for the Hawks. Kris Versteeg had a goal and two assists and Patrick Kane, Patrick Sharp, Brent Seabrook and Dave Bolland each had a goal and an assist for the Hawks.

Flyers defenseman Chris Pronger, a focal

Above: Michael Jordan watches Game 5 in the second period in the house that he built, the United Center. John J. Kim | Sun-Times

Versteeg scored. The production from Byfuglien, who had the secondary assists on Bolland's and Versteeg's goals, was just part of an overwhelming — and resilient — effort by the Hawks.

The fire was from everyone, and a show of a potential champion.

"Dustin was a piece of the 20 guys that went out there tonight and just wanted it," defenseman Brian Campbell said. "You got to have that attitude, where you want it more than them — and that team really wants it as well. Definitely in Philly, we lost a few battles that we should have won. Tonight, we won our fair share, and that's the difference."

The Hawks had more power plays than the Flyers in Game 5. They won more battles and were quicker to pucks. They controlled the tempo as their new lines, which included Jonathan Toews playing with Marian Hossa and Tomas Kopecky and Kane with Sharp and Andrew Ladd, clicked from the start.

The Flyers were able to make things interesting at times, cutting the Hawks' lead to two goals multiple times as Danny Briere, Scott Hartnell and Ville Leino continued to be threats.

But this time it was the Hawks who were able to respond with crucial goals. Byfuglien, Kane and Sharp answered with goals after Philadelphia scored.

"We knew we needed a big effort," Versteeg said. "We haven't brought it in the first four games, and tonight was the night we knew we needed to do it. We came out with a good effort, and that's the way we have to play moving forward."∎

point of media attention for his role in roughing up the Hawks without being called for penalties, was on the ice or in the penalty box for every goal scored by the Hawks. He was a minus-5 and was in the box when Byfuglien scored on the power play. The Hawks' first goal was a shot that deflected off Pronger on the power play.

"Getting down there two games in their building, we had to come back with some fire and just get on them and show them that we weren't going to quit," said Byfuglien, who sent Pronger crashing to the ice with a hit in the second period. "Right from the get-go we just moved our feet and stayed physical."

The get-go was a 3-0 lead after the first period as Seabrook (power play), Bolland and

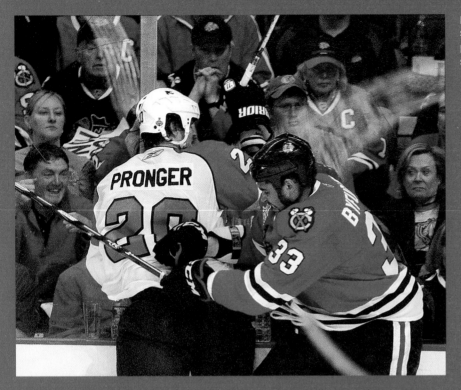

Forget the Blackhawks' pregame vow to play with desperation. That's the wrong word, and it doesn't do justice to what they did Sunday night.

They played with spirit. They played with attitude and resolve.

They played with everything they had.

They showed up in Game 5, the real Hawks did, and the result was a 7-4 victory that put them one game away from their first Stanley Cup in almost half a century.

Game 6 is Wednesday night in Philadelphia. Such a simple

declarative sentence. But you know better by now, don't you?

Desperation sounds so desperate. It diminishes what the Hawks were Sunday. They were all over the ice. They were wherever the puck was. They were on the Flyers like parkas on dogsledders.

They were great Sunday. Most of the time. OK, they were great when they weren't being overly protective with the lead.

But they were great.

Let's face it. Things had gotten grim around here. Confidence was shaken. People walked around town with eyes cast downward. Bullies couldn't work up the self-esteem to steal lunch money.

And the Hawks had to listen to people talk about the Flyers as the only team with a story to tell, a story of heart and grit. As if the Hawks couldn't do heart or grit.

'THIS IS WHAT IT'S ABOUT'

The shame about Games 3 and 4 was that the Blackhawks didn't come close to being the best they could be. It left them looking like a distant, unplugged team. Not what you want going into Game 5 of a tied series.

"We were flat-footed, it seemed, maybe a little nervous here and there," forward Kris Versteeg said of the first four games. "We said we were going to play our game Sunday, and that's what we did.

"Now we've got to keep that energy going into the next game and just have fun out there. This is what it's about. This is what we've played for since we were little."

The Hawks came out flying Sunday night, which is what Flyers are supposed to do, isn't it? Even though the first 12 minutes were

scoreless, the Hawks dominated the action, getting to almost every puck and treating the Philadelphia end as personal property.

A LITTLE MJ ALWAYS HELPS

And when the goals started coming, something like a great sigh of relief whooshed through the United Center, at a decibel level of about 115.

First Brent Seabrook on a shot off the skate of Flyers defenseman Chris Pronger that found the net.

Then Dave Bolland on a shot off the back of goalie Michael Leighton's skate.

Then a nasty Versteeg wrist shot.

Three goals in about six minutes.

There was a stoppage of play 20 seconds after Versteeg's goal, and the crowd of 22,305 stood and roared in appreciation. It had just witnessed a club at its best.

"Everybody on the team was battling," defenseman Duncan Keith said.

The most frustrating thing about the Hawks in the playoffs has been their tendency to go into a shell with a lead. It happened again in the second period.

The Flyers came out with fire, and the Hawks immediately stopped, dropped and rolled, allowing Scott Hartnell to tap in an easy one 32 seconds into the period.

Patrick Kane scored on Leighton's replacement, Brian Boucher, to make it 4-1. Breathing room, right? We're going to talk about the alchemy skills of coach Joel Quenneville, correct? How he put Kane with Andrew Ladd and Patrick Sharp? How the line of Bolland, Versteeg and Dustin Byfuglien had two goals in the first period?

Not so fast.

The Flyers scored one minute, 21 seconds later. Suddenly it was 4-2, and breathing passages were back to being constricted.

It was as if Philadelphia was on an extended power play, and the Hawks were just trying to stay above water. Someone needed to remind them they were in the lead.

Michael Jordan?

Sure, why not.

MJ was in the House He Built, and when the scoreboard showed him in a Toews jersey and waving a souvenir towel, there was more cheering. OK, you trot out Jordan, maybe you are desperate to make something happen.

Pronger, the Flagrant Flyer, soon after found himself in the penalty box, and it made all the difference for the Hawks.

Byfuglien scored on a tap-in to make it 5-2.

Pronger finished minus-five Sunday.

The Hawks can wrap this up in Philadelphia on Wednesday, but only if they arrive with the same vitality that helped them get through Sunday's ups and downs.

"We've got to come with our best effort," said center John Madden, who played on two Cup teams in New Jersey. "We've got to approach it like it's a Game 7 and it's do-or-die."

The Flyers say they're not dead, and the Hawks would be wise to believe it.

"One game is only one game," Philly coach Peter Laviolette said.

"There's usually not a carryover effect from game to game. You know, this is just one page of the story. Sunday, it was their page."

Here's chapter and verse: When the Hawks play hard, they're the better team. When they don't, they aren't.

Remember that, fellas. A Cup rides on your response.■

Above: Chicago Blackhawks, left to right, Dustin Byfuglien, Kris Versteeg and Partick Sharp skate back to the bench after scoring.
Scott Stewart | Sun-Times

Right: Dustin Byfuglien smiles after beating the Flyers 7-4 in Game 5.
John J. Kim | Sun-Times

Above: Brian Campbell, Patrick Kane and Patrick Sharp celebrate Kane's goal in the 2nd period. Tom Cruze | Sun-Times

★ THREE STARS ★

★ DUSTIN BYFUGLIEN
"Big Buff" came up big when his team needed him the most, producing the kind of stat line that can turn a player into a playoff hero. Byfuglien, who had one point in the first four games, had two goals, two assists and nine hits. Meanwhile, Flyers defenseman Chris Pronger, who has been his nemesis, finished with a minus-5 rating.

★ KRIS VERSTEEG
Versteeg set up a goal and scored another during the best first period the Hawks have played in the post-season. It was Versteeg's wrist shot at 18:15 of the first period that gave the Hawks a 3-0 lead they would not relinquish. He now has five points in the series.

★ VILLE LEINO
He continued to come up big in the postseason, delivering one of his best efforts. Even during the first period, when the Flyers were getting dominated, he excelled. He later would add three assists — two in the second period and one in the third - and now has points in eight of his last 11 games.

STANLEY CUP FINALS

GAME 6: BLACKHAWKS 4 | FLYERS 3 (OT)

The Blackhawks are the 2010 Stanley Cup champions.

They're no longer that team with the longest title drought in the NHL of 49 years.

They're no longer that fifth franchise in a crowded Chicago sports landscape of broken dreams and disappointment.

They're no longer that inept franchise that wallowed in mediocrity for years.

The Hawks are champions. They are the best.

They did it with a 4-3 victory in overtime over the never-out-of-it Philadelphia Flyers in Game 6 of the Stanley Cup finals Wednesday at the Wachovia Center.

The Hawks won it on Patrick Kane's game-winner 4:06 into overtime. They won it by using their depth and speed. They won it by overcoming adversity as champions do. They won it for the first time since 1961.

"This is something I'll never forget," Kane said. "I don't think it's really sunk in yet. This is just unbelievable to be a part of. I mean, we won the Stanley Cup."

Fittingly, it was Jonathan Toews, the Hawks' 22-year-old captain, who won the Conn Smythe Trophy as the most valuable player in the playoffs. Kane and Toews are the faces of the franchise.

With everything on the line, they were the Hawks' biggest players.

"This is the best feeling you can ever get playing hockey, and I just can't believe it's happening," Toews said. "I'm so excited to bring this home for our fans. But, most of all, we wanted to do it for each other."

After Toews was handed the Stanley Cup and he raised it, he gave it to winger Marian Hossa, who hoisted the Cup over his head for the first time after losing in the finals in consecutive seasons.

It also is Hawks coach Joel Quenneville's first Stanley Cup as a head coach.

"It's a great feeling," Quenneville said. "The party [in Chicago] is going to be unbelievable."

Andrew Ladd, Dustin Byfuglien (power play) and Patrick Sharp (4-on-4) also scored for the Hawks. Antti Niemi, the so-called question mark for the Hawks heading into the playoffs, made 21 saves, including huge stops on Jeff Carter and Claude Giroux with the game on the line.

Scott Hartnell was credited with the second biggest goal of the game with 3:59 left in the third, when Ville Leino's centering pass bounced around in front Niemi and off of Hossa and in.

It tied the game and highlighted the huge momentum swing by the Flyers and was the second of the game for Hartnell.

But destiny had the Hawks in mind as Kane's bad-angle shot with eyes from the bottom of the circle found a way past Michael Leighton (37 saves) in overtime.

The Hawks celebrated. The crowd was shocked. The goal was reviewed.

"I think I was the only one who knew it was in," Kane said.

The Flyers, who also got a goal from Danny Briere, were 9-1 at home this postseason head-

Above: Fans celebrate the Chicago Blackhawks Stanley Cup Championship at bars along Division Street on Wednesday night in Chicago.
Richard A. Chapman | Sun-Times

ing into Game 6, winning Games 3 and 4 of the finals over the Hawks.

The Hawks had also lost their last 10 games at the Wachovia Center.

But this year's version of the Hawks was never intimidated. They had done enough good things in Games 3 and 4 to believe that they could win at one of the more hostile places in the NHL.

The Stanley Cup title caps a remarkable turnaround by the Hawks, who had 65 points just a few years ago.

"It means everything. It's unbelievable just to see everybody on the ice, to see our families who supported us all year long," Sharp said. "I dreamed about holding [the Stanley Cup] my whole life — what a feeling."∎

The Blackhawks are the 2010 Stanley Cup champions.

Above the ice, the Stanley Cup gleamed and sparkled as it moved from new owner to new owner.

From Jonathan Toews, who was named most valuable player of the playoffs, to Marian Hossa, who had come so achingly close to a championship twice before, to Patrick Sharp, who had started his career in Philadelphia.

Now Brent Sopel and John Madden. Now Duncan Keith, the guy missing seven teeth, and his mate on defense, Brent Seabrook. And so on.

Above: Third time's the charm for Marian Hossa, who finally got to celebrate a Stanley Cup. Scott Stewart | Sun-Times

Opposite Page: Antti Niemi celebrates with the Stanley Cup. AP Photo

Finally Hawks owner Rocky Wirtz, the man who saw to the franchise's turnaround, handed the Cup to coach Joel Quenneville, who actually smiled. No, really. He did.

Pardon us if we're a little wide-eyed here. Many of us have never seen the Cup like this, in the hands of Blackhawks.

It looked different carried by men in Hawks jerseys. For Chicagoans who had experienced 49 years of desert dryness, it might as well have been space invaders hoisting the Cup.

When Patrick Kane knocked the puck under the legs of Philadelphia goalie Michael Leighton four minutes, six seconds into overtime Wednesday night, it gave the Hawks a 4-3 victory and handed the rest of the NHL a message.

Submit to the Indian.

The Flyers did, finally and inevitably. The

Hawks were the more talented team, and that was obvious for long stretches of Game 6. Their skating and passing were a thing of beauty, and in the end, there was nothing Philadelphia could about it.

Well, it could boo, which Flyers fans did loudly as the Hawks carried the Cup around the ice. You can't teach that kind of classiness. You're born with it.

For the Hawks, Wednesday's celebration was the culmination of a whirlwind three years.

"We've really come from not being very good a couple years ago to winning the Stanley Cup," Seabrook said. "I was joking around with a few of the trainers that you'd never think it would actually happen. I never did.

"It's unbelievable to bring the Cup back to

Chicago's great fans. We're going to have some parties with them."

There were stretches of frustration in this one. At times, the Hawks seemed intent on not making this easy for anyone except the Flyers.

With a 3-2 lead in the third period, they went into the hockey equivalent of the prevent defense. The damsel in distress was tied to the railroad tracks, and the hero was pacing over what to do.

It cost the Hawks. The Flyers' Ville Leino skated between two defenders and dumped the puck in front of the net. From there, it deflected off Hossa and onto the stick of Scott Hartnell, who knocked it past goalie Antti Niemi. Tie game. Silly.

Now the Flyers and their fans were totally engaged, their belief in manifest destiny total. The Hawks had allowed them to believe.

Overtime.

No problem. A little pain to go with your pleasure.

Kane's goal set off a delayed celebration. For a few seconds, no one seemed to be aware that the puck had gone in the net. Kane dropped his stick and gloves, and skated to the other end of the ice. The rest of the Hawks caught up with him and mobbed him.

"I saw it go right through the legs," Kane said. "Sticking right under the pad in the net. I don't think anyone saw it."

"It was kind of an awkward celebration," Toews said. "We didn't know what to do. We were all standing around for the official call.

"It didn't matter how it happened, how it went in."

There was a year of hard work and sacrifice in the wild celebration, and almost a half-century of frustration being released in it as well. The last time the Hawks won a Stanley Cup was in 1961. Were the 21-year-old Kane's parents even alive in 1961?

The Hawks came out blazing Wednesday night, as if all 49 of those years were fueling them.

There can't have been many other periods in which one team outplayed another so badly and still was locked in a 1-1 tie for its efforts. No offense to our friends in Philly — no, none at all — but the Flyers looked overmatched from the first faceoff. The Hawks' top line of Toews, Hossa and Tomas Kopecky was all over the place, and the energy seemed to set the tone for the other three lines.

The Hawks looked faster, stronger and better, probably because that's what they are. When Quenneville split up the line of Toews, Kane and Dustin Byfuglien before Game 5, it spread out the talent throughout the lines, and it quickly became apparent the Flyers couldn't keep up.

The first period Wednesday was simply an extension of that. The Hawks outshot the Flyers

17-7 and looked every bit that dominant.

It was the craziest game. For all the Hawks' decided advantages, the Flyers took a 2-1 lead on Danny Briere's second-period goal. It was made possible when Keith tripped on Hartnell's skate. The Hawks came back to score on a Sharp goal when both teams were down a man.

It was a 2-2 game that felt like a 4-2 Hawks lead. They knew they were the better team, even if the scoreboard didn't know it yet.

That finally changed when Andrew Ladd deflected a Niklas Hjalmarsson slap shot past Leighton to make it 3-2 in the second period.

That set up the maddening third period. And the third period set up the inevitable.

For Keith, all the struggles were worth it. So was the pain. He had lost seven teeth after being hit by a puck in the conference finals.

"I'll knock out all my teeth to hoist that thing again," he said, smiling that empty smile of his.

Before the game, the Flyers had handed out orange T-shirts with the slogan "Unfinished Business" printed on them. If, by unfinished business, they meant that sock drawers needed organizing in Philadelphia, well, yes, the city now has plenty of time to finish that business.■

Above: Blackhawks coach Joel Quenneville finally can smile after Patrick's Kane's overtime goal gave the Blackhawks their first Stanley Cup in 49 years. Scott Stewart | Sun-Times

★ THREE STARS ★

★ PATRICK KANE

The 21-year-old star cemented his legacy in Blackhawks lore with the most dramatic goal in the history of the franchise — scoring from a tough angle in overtime to end a 49-year Stanley Cup drought.

★ PATRICK SHARP

His steady production gets overshadowed by Patrick Kane and Jonathan Toews, but his contribution throughout the finals was invaluable. Scored a game-tying goal and a was a team-high plus-3.

★ ANTTI NIEMI

Not his best game of a stellar postseason, but as usual Niemi came up with the big saves when he absolutely had to have them to pave the way for Kane's game-winner in overtime. Stopped 21 of 24 shots. One of his biggest stops was when he stoned Simon Gagne on a breakaway early in the second period to keep the score at 1-1.

Above: The Blackhawks pose for a photograph with the Stanley Cup. John J. Kim | Sun-Times

Thank you, Blackhawks! Thank you so much!

Your sport was irrelevant.

Your sport was — by official use of the medical mirror under your puck-broken nose — one wheezy breath from dead.

Some of us have lived long enough to remember the championship from 1961. And we thought it would never happen again.

Why should it?

That last championship ended in April. There were six teams. Now there are 30.

Toews and Kane and Niemi and Buff and all the other guys — thank you!

In fact, you other guys — Bolland, Sharp, Hossa, Eager, Brouwer, Campbell, Fraser, Hjalmarsson, Kopecky, Ladd, Burish, Madden, Seabrook, Sopel, Versteeg — stand up and take repeated bows.

You guys showed us all that great hockey is created by teamwork. Not one of you is less worthy than any other.

That Patrick Kane scored the game-winner is astounding and right.

"I knew it went in right away," Kane said of the overtime goal. "What a feeling. I can't believe it. I can't believe this just happened. Holy crap. This is something you dream about as a kid, scoring the winning goal for the Stanley Cup."

I hope he can live with the honor and handle it well and proudly. Patrick, this is a rarity. This is a legacy.

Take the Stanley Cup, the huge winning goal, and make it grow into a tower of dignity.

Chicago buildings use lights to form a Stanley Cup and a message of support Wednesday night, June 9, 2010, after the Blackhawks defeated the Philadelphia Flyers 4-3 in Game 6 of the NHL Stanley Cup hockey finals. AP Photo

That this should be just the start of a dynasty for the Blackhawks — let's not even get into that.

"Someone had to be the hero," captain Toews said. "It happened to be Kaner. It doesn't matter who it was."

Forechecking? Fourth line? Dirty areas? Double blue lines?

We get it all now.

We love it.

Wait until the parade Friday, Blackhawks.

Chicago is ready.

"I saw the puck in the back of the net, and I said, 'Party's on.'" coach Joel Quenneville said. "The party is going to be unbelievable.

You'll feel the love, fellows.

You'll feel it from the educated city.∎